# PARTICIPATORY RURAL APPRAISAL AND QUESTIONNAIRE SURVEY

## STUDIES IN RURAL PARTICIPATION

No.1. Participatory Rural Appraisal Methodology and Applications
— *Neela Mukherjee*

No.2. Participatory Rural Appraisal and Questionnaire Survey Comparative Field Experience and Methodological Innovations
—*Neela Mukherjee*

No.3. Participatory Appraisal of Natural Resources
—*Neela Mukherjee*

*Forthcoming:*

* **Rural Habitat and Poverty: Whose Perceptions?**

---

**Dr. Neela Mukherjee** is currently employed as Professor of Economics at Lal Bahadur Shastry National Academy of Administration, Mussoorie. An alumna of the London School of Economics, London, Dr. Mukherjee's research interests are topical and varied. One ofher major areas of research is participatory development for which the present study. 'Participatory Rural Appraisal (PRA) and Questionnaire Survey: Comparative Field Experience and Methodological Innovations' is the second volume in the series, the first being 'Pariticipatory Rural Appraisal: Methodology and Applications'.

In her pursuit of participatory development, Dr. Mukherjee has undertaken action research, organised and conducted training courses in participatory methods and has directly conducted a large number of sessions with villagers and slum dwellers, in India and other countries. Her research background in quantitative economics and her field experience in PRA have helped to shape the analysis and many of the arguments offered in the present volume.

Her other professional interests relate to the political economy of greenhouse gases and multilateral negotiations for trade in services. The main thrust underlying her areas of interest is democratization of development process and empowerment of poor, implications of which are both in terms of empowerment of poor and deprived individuals and that of the poor countries of the South. Dr. Mukherjee has written and lectured extensively in her areas of interest and has a number of books and papers to her credit.

---

*Studies in Rural Participation - 2*

# PARTICIPATORY RURAL APPRAISAL AND QUESTIONNAIRE SURVEY

## (Comparative Field Experience and Methodological Innovations)

**NEELA MUKHERJEE**
Professor of Economics
L.B.S. National Academy of Administration
Mussoorie (Uttar Pradesh)
India

**CONCEPT PUBLISHING COMPANY, NEW DELHI 110059**

ISBN 81-7022-560-4 (HB)

First Published 1995
Reprinted 1997, 2003



*Published and Printed by*
Ashok Kumar Mittal
**Concept Publishing Company**
A/15-16, Commercial Block, Mohan Garden
NEW DELHI-110059 (India)

*Phones* : 25351460, 25351794
*Fax* : 091-11-25357103
*Email* : publishing@conceptpub.com

*The study is dedicated*
*to the villagers of*
*Krishna Rakshit Chak*
*and*
*Kalsigeriya*
*(District Midnapore, West Bengal, India),*
*from whom I learnt*
*my basic lessons in*
*Participatory Rural Appraisal*

# FOREWORD

The first half of the 1990s has witnessed the rapid, almost explosive invention and spread of new approaches and methods for inquiry, learning and empowerment. Those known as Participatory Rural Appraisal (PRA) have been described as a growing family of approaches and methods to enable local people to share, enhance and analyse their knowledge of life and conditions, to plan and to act. Innovation has been marked in different continents and countries, not least in East Africa, but much of the early innovation occurred in, and spread from, India. Activities described as PRA are now known in over 50 countries, including countries of the North which have learnt them from the South. PRA has taken many of us by surprise with its power, popularity and versatility.

PRA approaches and methods are pluralist. As this book shows, they are not exclusive. The philosophy of practitioners has usually been one of open sharing without boundaries, and of stressing the behaviour and attitudes of facilitators. PRA approaches and methods have certain core strengths. These usually entail: sitting down, listening, facilitating and learning; being open rather than closed; "handing over the stick", meaning passing the initiative (and sometimes literally the stick, or the pen, or the chalk) to local people; enabling people in groups to conduct their own analysis; visual representations made by groups, cumulatively built up and cross-checked, and taking forms such as maps, diagrams, matrices, listing and card sorting; counting, estimating, scoring and ranking; and making comparisons. As Dr. Mukherjee explains, the approaches and methods are based in a different paradigm from the questionnaire survey.

The speed of methodological development and spread has raised issues. One is that many of the leading PRA practitioners and trainers wish the term PRA, or "a PRA" to be limited to empowering processes which lead to participatory action at the local level, and do not wish it to be used to include activities which are primarily data collection by outsiders; Dr Mukherjee has met this point by using the phrase "PRA-type inquiry". Another concerns quality assurance in PRA and PRA-type inquiry, especially when so much of the practice is by people who are new to these.

And yet another set of issues, the subject matter of this book, is the comparison of questionnaire survey approaches and methods with those of PRA-type inquiry. For the first time, this book brings together and analyses evidence from different sources, considering whether and how PRA can or should be complementary or an alternative to questionnaires.

As Dr Mukherjee points out, these are early days. The experience and evidence are disparate and scattered. In bringing together what has been available, she has done a service in highlighting what has been found, and what remains to be learnt. As she points out, there remains scope for innovation, research on methodology, and further comparisons. This book should stimulate and encourage others to try out, invent, test and compare new methods. Those who do so will be able to share in the excitement of the quiet methodological revolution which is occurring, and to which this book provides a useful introduction.

18 January 1995

**Robert Chambers**
Institute of Development Studies,
University of Sussex
Brighton BNI 9 RE, UK

# PREFACE

After completion of my first volume on *Participatory Rural Appraisal (PRA): Methodology and Applications* in April 1993, I was looking for an opportunity to do further research in the area and it was not until the winter of 1993 that I got a chance to research on the second volume on PRA through a generous grant made by the Institute of Development Studies at the University of Sussex, and equally enabling infrastructural support from the Sustainable Agriculture Programme of the International Institute for Environment and Development, London.

This time, the focus of research was on comparing methods of data collection. Any exercise in data collection is based on a method/methods which involves/involve basic issues in cost, time, scale, utility, depth and trustworthiness of the data collected which vary with the method/methods used. My research focused on comparing conventional methods of investigation such as questionnaire survey with participatory methods like Participatory Rural Appraisal (PRA) as evolving from the field.

This was based on field experience across developing countries. PRA-type inquiry in use in different parts of the world led to interesting results which were accumulating from such studies. The series of experience from field situation on alternative systems of inquiry, especially on PRA were from a host of developing countries such as India, Nepal, Bangladesh, Sierra Leone, Pakistan and others. I researched on the recent empirical evidence, examined issues, looked at opportunities and analysed the methodological innovations made in field investigation and data collection.

The rich learning from the recent field experiences warrant a review of the methods for appreciating advancements in field studies and for learning how to improve methods of data collection. My learning experience is enriched in documenting, reviewing and analysing the field studies. In this study only those field experiences are reviewed which have either used both the conventional survey and PRA-type inquiry or have demonstrated 'scaling' up of PRA-type inquiry, thus performing much more than being confined to mere local level studies. Interestingly, most case studies have combined PRA-type inquiry with elements of the conventional survey method and have produced methodological innovations, many of which are novel in character, practical and can help to steer the course of future research in the field.

For any field investigation we generally have a methodology, a time schedule and a budget. Our objective is to arrive at the best possible set of data collected within a short period of time, and at a low budget. The recent field experiences show a variety of ways for collecting data with participatory techniques. However, in real life, conventional survey method still constitute the mainstay of data collection and overshadow the merits of other methods which tend to remain at the margin, discounted and disregarded by most professionals. It is in this context that the study projects certain learning points from the field.

The book is divided into five chapters. In Chapter 1, two systems of inquiry, the conventional questionnaire survey and the PRA-type inquiry have been defined, illustrated and compared in terms of their paradigmatic bases, principles, objectives and ways of evaluating data. In Chapter 2, there are 11 case studies from the developing world showing how greater flexibility can be induced in field situation by adopting PRA method for data collection and analysis of local people's criteria. Chapter 3 deals with the issue of PRA method as a complement to questionnaire survey while in Chapter 4, PRA method is posed as an alternative to questionnaire survey. With a spectrum of experience from the field, different aspects of PRA-type inquiry have been examined in order to draw interim conclusions on comparative issues like cost, time, training, scale of inquiry, process, flexibility, depth, utility, trustworthiness, empowerment and learning. Chapter 5 presents the summary and conclusions of the study and also draws up a checklist for conducting a participatory nature of field inquiry.

For professionals engaged in conventional survey, the message from the field is that any conventional survey can be better informed when combined with PRA-type inquiry. For PRA specialists, field experience indicates that the flexibility inherent in PRA approach can be gainfully utilised for combining it with other methods for scaling up of data and arriving at overviews. Some of the questions on comparative 'cost' associated with the two systems of inquiry remain partially answered. We look forward to more and better field experience and await other results to arrive from the field. In the meanwhile, we have enough field results to improve upon our methods of data collection exercises, making them more flexible, innovative and useful.

I am grateful to Dr. Robert Chamber and Dr. Jules Pretty for their encouragement towards researching in this area and their comments on the draft of the study. I express my sincere thanks to those who read parts of the draft and offered their comments, foremost amongst them are Dr. Ian Scoones, Irene Guijt, Dr. Yvonne Rydin and Devika Tamang. I must also thank John Thompson, Parmesh Shah, Sheelagh Stewart, Dr. S.K. Chowdhury, Humeira Malik and Dr. Abel Rajaratnam for their suggestions. My thanks are also due to Helen Mclaren, Ginny Tim, Lynette Spence, Elainne Morrison and Patricia Bond for their support towards my research.

My sincere thanks are due to my husband Dr. Amitabha Mukherjee for his comments, views and suggestions relating to chapters 1 and 3 of this book and to my son Taponeel who patiently and ungrudgingly bore all inconveniences during my writing of this book. I am solely responsible for any error and omission in this study.

I am thankful to Dr. Robert Chambers for agreeing to write the foreword to this book in the midst of his busy schedule.

I also owe my thanks to Ashok Mittal of Concept Publishing Company for publication of this book.

I hope the book is useful to the practitioners of PRA, to students of field-methods, to those involved in data collection exercise and to policy-makers associated with international, national and regional statistical systems.

**8th November, 1994** **Neela Mukherjee**
**Dehradun**

# CONTENTS

# EXECUTIVE SUMMARY

Data collection in field level investigations need not be a monotonous and a routine exercise. It can be quick, interesting and innovative and at the same time be participatory, representative and trustworthy. In recent times, there has been a series of experience from field situation on alternative systems of inquiry, especially in Participatory Rural Appraisal (PRA)-type inquiries. As an alternate approach to data collection, such experience has helped in demonstrating PRA's potential in performing much more than just being confined to local level studies. Field evidence on PRA-type inquiries as a way to generate quick and meaningful data is growing over the years. The methodology of PRA, however, is much more than mere collection of data. It is essentially a way of people's participation, involving process, techniques and leading to people's action based on such process. In any PRA exercise, one important output from the process is generation of data. In this study, I focus on the use of PRA-type inquiries as a means of data collection for a comparison with the conventional questionnaire survey.

The book compares conventional methods of investigation such as questionnaire survey with participatory methods like Participatory Rural Appraisal (PRA) as evolving from the field. Of late, there has been a series of experience from field situation on alternative systems of inquiry, especially on PRA. They relate to a host of developing countries such as India, Nepal, Bangladesh, Sierra Leone, Pakistan and others. The book analyses the recent empirical evidence, examines issues, looks at opportunities and suggests potential for methodological innovations in field investigation and data collection.

Interesting results are accumulating from the field which show the following:

* PRA data are information-loaded, quick and participatory.
* Use of PRA-type inquiry for data collection involving larger scales (than was thought possible in recent past) is gaining evidence.
* Generation of PRA data through field learning is growing and

is being adapted to different ways of evaluation and cross-checking for judging its trustworthiness.

In other words, trends in field experience are indicative that PRA-type inquiry is steadily moving towards replication of its performance in terms of scale, magnitude, variety, quickness and validity. Based on results from various quarters, such kind of inquiry holds rich potential as a methodology for data collection. The ideal situation in this context is a combination of its innate qualities of analysing differences, diversities and people's involvement in data generation together with scaling up of data on a regional or a national basis. With the above in the background, the question is whether field experience provides enough indication for PRA-type inquiry to be considered as an alternative or a complementary methodology to questionnaire survey, the conventional method for data collection.

The present study is an attempt to compare conventional methods of investigation like questionnaire surveys with participatory methods like PRA-type inquiries as evolving in recent years. PRA method has been widely demonstrated to work well at community level but the future challenge lies in its scale of inquiry, whether it can work equally efficiently at the meso or the macro level. The recent empirical evidence raises issues, opportunities and opens up potential for methodological innovations.

The book is divided into five chapters. In Chapter 1 two systems of inquiry, the conventional questionnaire survey and the PRA-type inquiry have been defined, illustrated and compared in terms of their paradigmatic bases, principles, objectives and ways of evaluating data. In Chapter 2, there are 11 case studies from the developing world showing how greater flexibility can be induced in field situations by adopting PRA method for data collection and analysis of local people's criteria. Chapter 3 deals with the issue of PRA method as a complement to questionnaire survey while in Chapter 4, PRA method is posed as an alternative to questionnaire survey. With a spectrum of experience from the field, different aspects of PRA-type inquiry have been examined in order to draw interim conclusions on comparative issues like cost, time, training, scale of inquiry, process, flexibility, depth, utility, trustworthiness, empowerment and learning. Chapter 5 presents the summary and conclusions of the study and also draws up a check list for conducting a participatory nature of field inquiry.

In short, the major aspects covered by the present study are as follows:

* analysis of the issues from recent field experience which

encourage a comparison of PRA-type inquiry with questionnaire survey;

* interim appraisal of methodological innovations emerging from field experience;
* the larger context of paradigmatic bases, principles, objectives, operational issues and contextual basis of data involved in the two systems of inquiry under consideration;
* scanning the scope for evaluating/judging data from PRA-type inquiry, its attributes relating to the kind of data, representativeness, independence, trustworthiness and output;
* identification of certain gaps to be filled in this regard by PRA practitioners so as to have more and better evidence from new field experience; and
* suggest a check-list for approaching field level inquiry.

The above aspects of data collection are expected to go a long way in exploring, validating and reinforcing, if any, the position of PRA-type inquiry as a methodology for data collection whether as complement or a substitute to that of conventional questionnaire survey.

# 1

# INTRODUCTION

The prerogative of questionnaire survey and its use in data collection continues unabated in the methodological domain of applied field studies and research not withstanding the fact that in the history of methodological debates the analytic problems in questionnaire survey have raised fundamental doubts about the quality and credibility of survey results. One study (Gill: 1993) reporting on problems of official statistics based on surveys concludes that many such statistics are characterized by unreliability, gaps, over-aggregation, inaccuracies, mutual inconsistencies and untimely reporting. Policy formulation based on such incorrect empirical data lead to wrong decision-making. Questionnaire surveys can systematically understate or conceal different earnings/activities for instance, by asking respondents to state only the principal source of external earnings over preceding year (Breman: 1985). Data generated by macro surveys is mistaken for reality and what cannot be measured is either ignored or denied (Chambers: 1986). However, in absence of appropriate methods to handle our methodological requirements we have chosen to ignore the fallacies/ pitfalls associated with the questionnaire survey.

## Survey Data

In recent years, investigative research has offered great scope for methodological innovations as a result of which alternative systems of inquiry are being appreciated and made operational in field situation; they are being shaped and polished for professional use even when the survey's dominance as the uncrowned king continues. Moris (1970) has neatly summed up the problems of a formal survey associated with sampling, response of respondents, survey staff, recording inaccuracy and the common types of interview errors. The dominance of survey data can be explained as a mix of convenience and compulsion. Gill (1993) lists the compelling reasons for using official statistics gathered through survey. They are in terms of:

* ready availability—sometimes raw data and sometimes machine-readable format;
* cheap and easy to use since no data collection exercise is involved;
* wide coverage suited to a macro-level analysis; and
* official sanction since they are published by the government.

In this context, the question is whether we chose to ignore and brush aside our methodological problems or continue our search for better and richer alternatives. The answer to the question depends on empirical evidence from the field. Today, we see some hope in the direction of methodological improvement given the encouraging results from the field on participatory inquiry especially in the context of Participatory Rural Appraisal (PRA) method. It is important to assess the direction of change, its effectiveness and the way it is moving.

Not very long ago, we as outsiders visiting local communities found it impossible to believe that respondents to questionnaires were capable of not merely responding to our questions but could also pose their own questions and make us learn much more in terms of their analysis, their priorities and experiences. In recent years, there has started re-thinking on methodological issues and major paradigmatic shifts. These have provided the opportunity to think, apply and test the methodology of participatory inquiry, independently of the conventional questionnaire survey and interestingly enough, these developments in the field have been mostly in the countries of the South. In this context, PRA has been in the forefront of experiments and innovations to provide a better framework to people to generate their own data, plan, implement and evaluate their own activities and programmes. It, thus marks a departure, from the conventional setting where the people are used as respondents by enumerators for extractive generation of data through questionnaires designed by researchers in their own mode of analysis.

The present study compares conventional methods of investigation like questionnaire surveys with participatory inquiries of PRA-type as evolving in recent years. The recent empirical evidence raises issues, opportunities and opens up potentials in the field of methodological innovations. It is an interim appraisal of methodological innovations emerging from field experience in the context of a comparative evaluation of paradigmatic bases, principles, objectives, operational issues, contextual basis and validity of data involved in the two methodologies of PRA and questionnaire survey. In addition to this, the study also examines the validity of a few common doubts generally raised against PRA method and discusses certain gaps to be filled in this regard by PRA practitioners so as to have more and better evidence from new field experience.

However, not all methodological issues are easy to resolve since answers to comparing different dimensions of the two methodologies are expected to emerge from natural settings and not from laboratory experiments. Based on evidence flowing from field experience in PRA-type inquiries it may be said that some of the answers are gradually evolving while others are yet to emerge from the field. In any case, it is worth pursuing an interim analysis of the issues in the debate so as to score the rating of the progress made in this direction and also to look for viable options to data generation.

## Conventional Methodology

The conventional survey method is a commonly used method for data collection. It involves surveying of a selected area by means of a wide variety of instruments such as filling of questionnaires, interviewing (whether by means of telephone or otherwise), directly observing, measuring or combining all of them. Survey method is generally the accepted method of data collection and used both on a large and small scale. A survey can be through a sample survey or that of complete enumeration.

In a wider sense, Scherr *et al.* (1992) lists basic survey approaches and distinguishes them on the basis of (a) full coverage of population like census, vital statistics and remote sensing; (b) selection of representative study units by using statistical sampling techniques such as multi-visit household survey and single-visit household survey and (c) other approaches which make no attempt at drawing statistical sampling frame but try to understand the general character or dynamics of an issue such as Rapid Rural Appraisal, case studies and community interviews. In this study, however, we focus on the instrument of questionnaire as used in the survey method which can be for a census or a sample survey and involve single-visit or multi-visit to household as compared to a participatory type of inquiry.

### *Census*

Complete enumeration is applied for census data and involves enumeration of all subjects covered by the area of the survey and by nature such investigation does not permit any exclusion. Examples of complete enumeration are population census, economic census, livestock census and agricultural census which provide numerical picture of the concerned subject existing at the time of the census. Such surveys are important in their own way for political, constitutional and administrative requirement for separate figures describing the main features of the population for each of the smallest administrative units of the government. In this sense, the population census operation provides a national inventory, a picture of the situation existing at the time of the census. A brief description of the sample survey follows.

*Sample Surveys*

A sample survey can be applied to a village, town, district, region or a country or countries. It can be small, medium or large in size and cover households/individuals/firms/other units. It can be on a single subject or on multiple subjects. The collection of data may be:

* through filling up of a questionnaire,
* through measurement, e.g. for estimated measurement of crops and forests surveys,
* through interviews,
* through observation of respondents or the phenomenon under study, and/or
* through some combination of these procedures.

Sample survey is a flexible method and suits the requirements of data collection in respect of an universe which is large in size and for which complete coverage or enumeration is either difficult or expensive. It meets the needs of circumstances where inferences about the universe are required, and a census is neither possible nor desirable for different reasons such as cost and time. It also has three advantages over complete enumeration, economy of cost both in terms of time and money, since only a limited number of units from the universe have to be examined and analysed; it can lead to better accuracy resulting from better quality of enumeration and supervision as compared to census; and adaptable to the investigation of several issues, particularly those involving detailed transactions of individuals or households requiring an intensity of interview or observation. This may not be possible to achieve in census operation.

*The Questionnaire Survey*

The most widely used method for collecting socio-economic data is that of questionnaire survey which entails administering a written questionnaire to respondents. Such surveys can be done at one point of time or periodically.

A questionnaire can be defined as a group of questions designed to elicit information upon a subject, or a sequence of subjects, from a set of respondents. With regard to questionnaires used by an enumerator in interviewing respondents, the design of the questionnaire is deliberately simplified in order to have a wide-ranging applicability to the area/areas concerned.

It partakes the nature of an 'in- house' document and the explanations of concepts and discussions of procedure are provided to the enumerators during their briefing sessions and/or training course.

A standardised questionnaire survey generally reflects the following features:

* a substantial part of the conversation consists of questions and answers;
* the participants have defined non-over lapping roles where one person questions while the other answers; and,
* the product of the survey is generally quantitative or numerical figures describing characteristics of the population.

Data and measures to be analysed are the answers given by the respondents. The standard for the success of a survey is how well the data measures the aspects of the population the researcher is trying to describe (Fowler and Mangione:1990).

*Illustration of Questionnaire Survey from Field*

Here is a glimpse of a Questionnaire used for conducting Household Survey in India. This is done with a view to assess income groups of rural households amongst others.

A close examination of the above questionnaire shows that it collects data on the characteristics of a household in question as measured by its agricultural land, agricultural equipments, condition of housing, livestock, properties, income, loans, beneficiary of government programmes etc. and on that basis assesses the income group of the household concerned.

## Why Another Methodology?

In recent years, the area of development is undergoing paradigmatic shifts from 'development from above' to that from 'below'. It is being increasingly

**Table 1.1**

*HOUSEHOLD SURVEY ANNEXURE*

**Annual Income (in Rupees):**

| | | |
|---|---|---|
| | (0-4000) | Caste:........................ |
| | (4001-6000) | |
| | (6001-8500) | Category:........................ |
| | (8501-11000) | |
| 1. | Name:........................... Development Block:................ | 4. Hamlet:.................... |
| 2. | Nyaya Panchayat:.................... | 5. Village:.................... |
| 3. | Gram Sabha:......................... | 6. Village Code:................ |
| 7. | Name of the Head of the Househol:.................................................. | |
| 8. | Details of Members of the Household:................................................ | |
| 9. | Total Agricultural Land owned by the Household (ha) :.............. | Irrigated/Unirrigated/Means of Irrigation |
| 10. | Details of Agricultural Equipments: | Tractor/Pump Set/Electric Tube Well/ Thresher/Others |
| 11. | Whether Household owns a House ?: | *Kutcha*/*Pucca*/Approximate Area/ Adequate/Inadequate Indira Awas/ Year of Construction |
| 12. | Livestock: | Number............/Approximate Price/ ........... |
| 13. | Details of Other Properties: | Radio/TV/Refrigerator/ Cooker/ Sofa Set/Bed/Others |
| 14. | Income (in Rupees) from Agricultural Labour/Other: | Agriculture/Livestock/Labour/Employment/Industry/Occupation/Rents/Total |
| 15. | Household Loan: | Objective/Year/Position of Payment/ Personal/Moneylender (Accounts)/ Cooperative Bank Rural/Commercial Bank |
| 16. | Whether the Household received Benefit from IRDP Scheme Earlier: | Name/Year/Scheme/Loan/Grant/ Member Present/Condition of Assets/ Position of Repayment/The Assets |
| | Whether this resulted in the improvement of the position of the household ? If yes, increase in the annual income :............................................................. | |
| 17. | Whether any Member of the Household wants benefit from IRDP Scheme. If yes, which Scheme ........................ Name of Members .................. | Available Infrastructure/ Facility in the village for the sake of the Scheme |
| 18. | Whether any Member of the Household wants to be trained under TRYSEM..... If yes, the name of the Trade in which interested to be trained:........................ | |

appreciated by policy-makers, planners, administrators and donor agencies that until and unless the local communities can participate in their own development programmes such programmes administered by outside agencies remain 'exogenous' to the rural community which in turn, can adversely affect the results of such programmes. Indigenous knowledge system constitutes an alternative model for sustainable development. It is the sum total of experience and knowledge of a given group that can be used to form the basis for decision-making in the face of familiar and unfamiliar problems and challenges (Warren and Cashman: 1988).

Questionnaire survey constitutes a system of inquiry where the questionnaire is in a mode of 'development from above'. Designed by specialists, it basically reflects their 'worldview' or perceptions of the topic to be probed by means of the questionnaire. The respondents act as passive entities and merely answer the questions thought to be important and relevant by those designing and canvassing the questionnaire.

One way to narrow the gap between local communities and outside professionals is by getting closer to local people and learning from them. By 'getting closer' is meant establishing better rapport and improved channels of communications. For this purpose, the attitudes have to be congenial to that of learning and of embracing errors for which the conventional methods for learning about them would have to undergo significant changes with the objective of empowering the local people to do their own analysis and take decisions influencing their own well being.

**What is Participatory Rural Appraisal ?**

Participatory Rural Appraisal (PRA) is a methodology which helps in interacting with local communities, understanding them and learning from them. It helps in the process of involvement with local communities for indigenous knowledge-building exercises. It is a way of learning from and with community members to investigate, analyze and evaluate constraints and opportunities and make informed and timely decisions regarding development projects.

It involves a set of principles, a process of communication and a menu of techniques for seeking villagers' participation in putting forward their points of view about any issue and enabling them do their own analysis and offer their own contribution in different forms with a view to make use of such learning. It initiates a participatory process and sustains it. Its principles and the menu of techniques help in organizing participation.

PRA is a means of generating different kinds of data, identifying and mobilising intended groups and evoking their participation and also opening ways in which intended groups can participate in decision making, project design, execution, monitoring and evaluation. It provides an alternative framework for data collection and analysis. Because of its participatory nature, it is an useful methodology to focus attention on people, their livelihoods and their inter-relationships with socio-economic and ecological factors.

PRA is sometimes known as Rapid Rural Appraisal (RRA)/Participatory Rapid Appraisal (PRA) where the emphasis is on both 'rapid' and 'participatory'. The emphasis on 'rapid' however, is more in terms of data collection and less in terms of the process of development or even implementation of plans. Other names are also used for describing PRA, some of which are Participatory Rapid Rural Appraisal (PRRA) and Participatory Learning Method (PALM). PRA, as practised in the field has given rise to different schools of PRA with difference in style and emphasis (Chambers: 1991).

*An Illustration of Participatory Rural Appraisal Inquiry for Wealth Grouping*

The following account provides an illustration of a PRA-type session on technique of wealth grouping where village communities grouped households in their villages on the basis of their criteria of poverty and wealth (Mukherjee: 1993). Such exercises of wealth grouping were conducted in three villages named Kalsigeriya, Berapal and Krishna Rakshit Chak in Midnapore District of West Bengal, India.

The normal process was to draw the villagers together near a village school or a tea stall or some other common location and explain to them the reason for visiting their village. The reason as stated was for the purpose of research in order to know more about the villagers, their indigenous knowledge and their perceptions on poverty and wealth. Generally the villagers were enthusiastic to gather together and meet the outsiders and exchange their views. At the beginning mostly the male residents of the village and the children gathered. After some time, the female residents also joined the group and closely observed the other villagers before reacting.

To begin with, it was a session of rapport-building with the villagers introducing oneself and knowing their names. Then the villagers were asked to describe their village and their day to day living so that the visitors from outside could know more of them. Gradually the villagers of the three villages described above were requested to draw map of their individual village including the households and land-use patterns and explain it on that basis. The mapping technique was used to elicit community responses in identifying the different groups of rich and poor and grouping them accordingly. The entire exercise of mapping and wealth grouping was done by the villagers. On average, the villagers took around three to four hours to map the entire village and explain the basis of grouping of households. Both men and women participated in explaining the map they made and in case of differences of opinion the villagers were able to sort them out amongst themselves through intense discussions.

The PRA techniques of mapping and grouping of village households were used by the villagers to identify the different socio-economic strata of households, group them and to identify the 'poorest of the poor' and move upwards to other groups. In this process, the villagers were also able to explain the criteria used for such grouping of different households.

First, the villagers mapped their entire village on a paper with a pencil. Then they identified the 'poorest of the poor' households in the village by marking those households on the map through symbols (see Fig. 1.1). They also described the characteristics and reasons which made these households lie at the bottom line of poverty.

The villagers then identified the next group of poor households which had a higher rank along with the specific conditions and characteristics. For the purpose of such grouping, the question posed to the villagers was: "Which households were slightly better than the 'poorest of the poor' and what were their characteristics ?"

The villagers marked each set of households differently with different symbols. They distinguished between different layers of poor households ranking them from bottom and enumerating their characteristics until all households in the village were covered. As and when the different layers of households were identified the villagers used coloured pens in order to distinguish between the different kinds of households, the land use patterns and other resources in the village.

### *Indigenous Criteria of Wealth and Poverty*

The villagers seemed to have a mental checklist which they were referring to for grouping of households, the checklist for determining their criteria for well-being. They identified poor households on the basis of the conditions and causes of poverty prevailing in such households. Food availability including wild food, during a year was the most significant factor for the villagers in grouping of poor households. The size of landholdings and its productivity

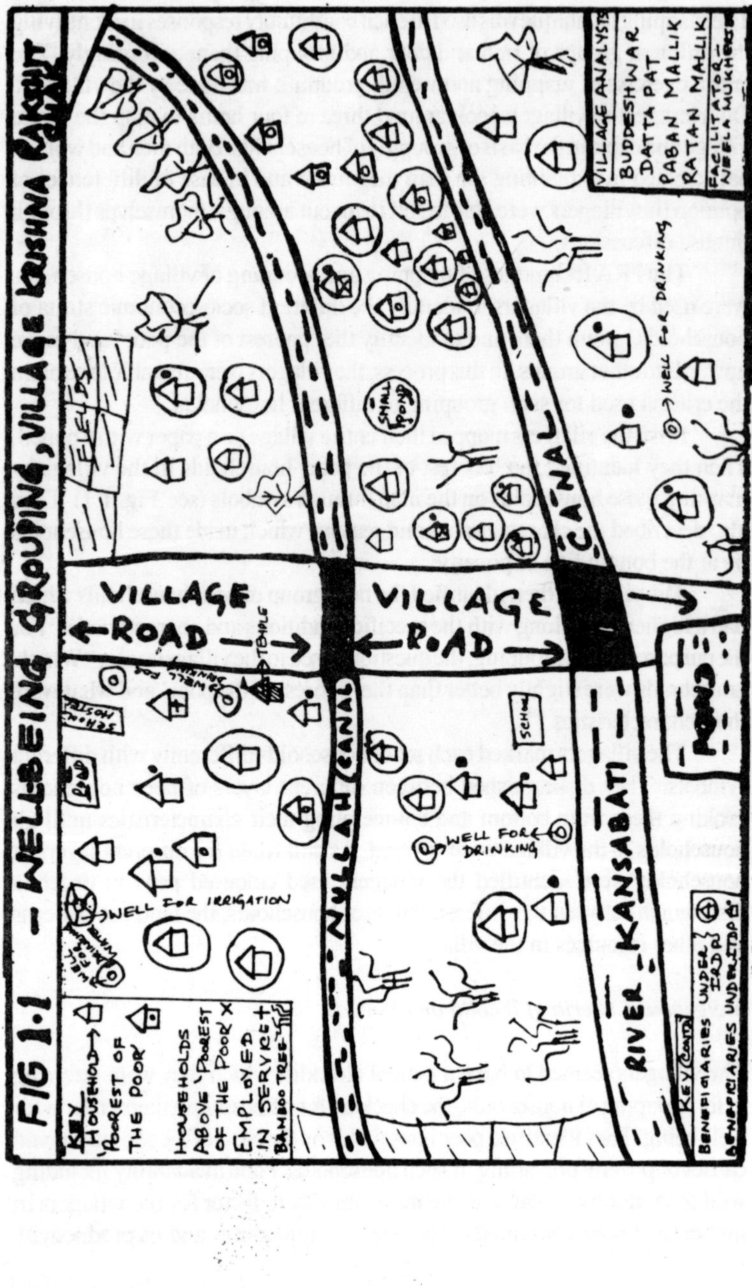
FIG 1·1 – WELLBEING GROUPING, VILLAGE KRISHNA
KEY
HOUSEHOLD → 'POOREST OF THE POOR'
HOUSEHOLDS ABOVE 'POOREST OF THE POOR' X
EMPLOYED IN SERVICE +
BAMBOO TREE
WELL FOR IRRIGATION
POND
FIELDS
VILLAGE ROAD
TEMPLE
WELL FOR DRINKING
SMALL POND
NULLAH (CANAL)
CANAL
RIVER KANSABATI
POND
VILLAGE ANALYSTS
BUDDESHWAR
DATTA PAT
PABAN MALLIK
RATAN MALLIK
FACILITATOR
NEELA MUKHERJEE
KEY (CONTD)
BENEFICIARIES UNDER IRDP

was another important consideration for the villagers for identifying higher groups but land alone was not enough. Its productive capacity was equally important. The number of dependents was also another consideration apart from food availability and land holdings.

On the basis of semi-structured interviews the reasons for poverty and deprivation were highlighted by the villagers. Environmental degradation had accentuated the uncertainty of food availability from common property resources and increased the incidence of poverty. Common property resources lent support in several ways. For many, such resources formed the basis of their livelihood, for others it supplemented income, food and other requirements and also provided sustenance during difficult times. Environmental degradation had reduced the quality of life for the poor. It had led to increased deprivation. The poor were no longer able to fall back on the environment for food, water, work, medicines, fuelwood and clean air especially during lean periods and in years of crop failures. The degradation of ponds, pastures, river beds, decline in the number of trees and shrubs, decline in area, decline in quality of water and the erosion of forests as sources of food, fodder and fuelwood had directly affected their sources of livelihood, cost of living, its standards, costs and health.

### *A Comparison of the Illustrations of Questionnaire Survey and PRA Technique of Wealth Grouping*

In this section, I shall compare the illustrations of questionnaire survey as in Table 1.1 and PRA wealth grouping as described above. Both of them have a common objective of categorising households in villages based on socio-economic criteria. The questionnaire survey does them on the basis of set standards which are pre-determined by researchers while, in PRA, socio-economic grouping of households is done by the villagers on the basis of their criteria. The factors considered important for economic grouping of households by the questionnaire are different from those considered by the villagers. Socio-economic grouping is based on income of different groups as estimated on the basis of the data provided by the questionnnaire whereas in PRA method it is done by local people based on their criteria and is in the nature of relative grouping based on consensus.

* The questionnaire has accounted for the major characteristics associated with different income groups, however, the processes which make for those characteristics have not been included as questions in the questionnaire. The PRA illustration on socio-

economic grouping shows how the causal process underlying those characteristics are important and can also be accounted for.

* The questionnaire is limited to a fixed set of questions which are uniformly canvassed. To give one instance, fixed questions are asked on house, income, property, livestock, loan etc. For facilitating quantification of responses it has also been observed that standard estimates are provided from outside. For example in the questionnaire survey, income flow from livestock is provided as an estimate from the 'top' for assessment of income categories. It creates virtually little scope for including those contextual/local characteristics thought to be important by local people and which make for considerable differences in income groups of rural households. For instance, as indicated in question no.9 of the questionnaire, the quality of land, its kind of soil and moisture content/crops grown/ position of land are not of any consideration in the questionnaire although field experience shows that the villagers find them to be important factors determining their income. One reason for such omission may be to limit the number of questions to only those aspects considered important by the outside investigators.
* Socio-economic grouping of households through assessment of annual income is directly based on estimates made by the enumerators in terms of questions asked. Such grouping of households into different income groups is fixed in terms of a 'blue-print' for income classification, imposed from the 'top' in which the local people's perceptions and their knowledge are missing. In case of PRA method the illustration shows how the local people use their criteria to determine different socio-economic groups in their villages.
* The aspect of seasonal income has also been overlooked in the questionnaire for household survey and average income has been arrived at by smoothening of daily and seasonal fluctuations and through approximations of wages/earnings/returns from assets. The illustration of PRA method shows how seasonal component is an important variable. For example, seasonal food availability during a year determined grouping of poor households. Seasons can play an important role in determining livelihoods at the local level and hence any realistic assessment need to include seasons. The two illustrations of questionnaire survey and PRA wealth grouping as given above, indicate that there are basic differences

in the two approaches with regard to their forms, their theories, their modes of operation, their objectives, process, techniques and output. With this in background we can look for a comparative picture of the two systems of inquiry relating to their paradigmatical bases, principles, objectives and other dimensions.

## Comparative Analysis: Paradigms, Principles, Objectives and Evaluation

It is important that any analysis of evidence and experience concerning PRA-type inquiry and questionnaire survey is preceded by a discussion of the foundations of the two systems of inquiry under review. This would help in understanding and appreciating the underlying differences, if any, of the two systems in the context of their paradigmatic bases, principles, objectives and ways of evaluation. This would also constitute a base for reviewing field experience under the two systems of inquiry.

Any inquiry whether through questionnaire survey or PRA would be guided by their respective basic belief systems which are known as paradigms. Each paradigm responds to three basic questions concerning the nature of reality (ontology), the nature of relationship between the knower and the known (epistemology) and the methodology involved (Guba:1990). In this Chapter, I examine the two systems of inquiry, the questionnaire survey and the PRA method on the basis of the following criteria:

* Paradigmatic Basis
* Principles
* Objectives
* Evaluation of Data

### *Paradigmatic Basis and Positivism*

The methodologies of questionnaire survey and PRA emerge from different paradigms. The differences in their paradigmatic bases are a key to understanding the diversities in the nature of systems of inquiry and their practice. To quote Schwandt (1990), "to study a methodology is not simply to examine the exercise of method, it is to study a way of knowing......to explore a logic of justification or a meta-framework for understanding the exercise of method, that is for examining the principles and procedures by which we formulate inquiry problems, and evaluate the correctness and profundity of those answers."

Positivism constitutes the basic belief system of conventional inquiry in which lies the paradigmatic basis of the questionnaire-survey. The nature of reality of positivism constitutes reality which exists 'out there' and is driven by immutable natural laws and mechanisms. Its nature of relationship between the knower or inquirer and the known is that of an objectivist. It is both possible and essential for the inquirer to adopt an objective approach to the inquiry.

The methodology of positivism is scientific. Questions and hypotheses are posed in advance in forms of propositions and are subjected to empirical testing under carefully controlled conditions. To state it in simple words, the scientific methodology is principally concerned with procedures for the development and testing of causal hypotheses. The cornerstones of the methodology lie in observation, measurement, experiment, and theory building with statistics playing a major role in formulation and testing of hypotheses.

In social disciplines, our understanding of methodology has been generally based on the conception of scientific inquiry, the principles and procedures that govern investigations of the physical world. In line with this, our professional belief in the naturalistic interpretation of social sciences is also pronounced. We regard the scientific methodology as a sure and an independent way of being rational in our inquiry.

*Paradigm Blockade and Post-positivism*

Any paradigm can block the level of inquiry in four ways:

* absolute assertion
* the claim that certain things can never be known
* the claim that certain elements of science are basic and independent of all else
* the claim that a law or truth has found its last and perfect formulation.

In the emerging era of post-positivism, such claims of positivism are being increasingly challenged in social disciplines. The methodology of natural sciences is being questioned and being replaced by methods drawn from humanistic disciplines. In this context, post-positivism recognises that many imbalances of positivism have been allowed in the name of achieving realistic and objective inquiry. Some of them are as follows:

* The imbalance between rigour and relevance, where, search for more rigour to establish internal validity make the findings less

generalized. Thus the laboratory results are generalizable only to another laboratory.

* The imbalance between precision and richness which leads to overemphasis on quantitative methods and precise and accurate responses.
* The imbalance between discovery and verification which leads to acceptibility of selected results since there are not many objective ways of verifying all kinds of results.
* The imbalance between elegance and applicability where the emphasis is on the statement of formal and reductionist theories and their testing and applications. Such theories may not be appropriate in the local context thus making elegant theories redundant and unrealistic.

## THE CONSTRUCTIVIST PARADIGM

The history of science and inquiry reveals that our knowledge of both the external world and the ways and means of human interaction is always evolving (Schwandt: 1990). Hence some paradigms become old while others are relatively new and emerging. One such recent paradigm is that of constructivist paradigm. Methodologies of such paradigm aim at understanding as much as possible the following:

* Aspects of human experience as it is lived or felt or undergone as participants in that experience
* The context of that experience
* The naturally occurring context
* Procedures for considering the context and the experience as a complex, temporal, socio-cultural and geographic whole
* The inquirer employing ordinary field-work methods

The constructivist methodologies reject the naturalistic interpretation of the social sciences and aim at inquiring and interpreting the realm of inter-subjective meaning as constituted in culture, language, signs, symbol etc. One contribution to systems of inquiry from the constructivist paradigm is the emergence of participatory inquiry whose framework of analysis is constructive rather than naturalistic.

## THE PARADIGM OF 'CRITICAL REALISM'

The paradigm of 'critical realism' is another development in the era of postpositivism from which participatory inquiry has routed its evaluation of findings. The nature of reality is such that the inquirer needs to be critical about findings because of human limitations regarding knowledge of reality. Critical realism recognises that findings emerge from the interaction of inquirer and inquired and hence proposes a modified objectivity by relying on 'critical tradition' which implies that report on any inquiry needs to be consistent with the existing tradition of the field and subjects every inquiry to peer group judgement in the 'critical community'. This makes it difficult for old and new paradigms to assert themselves.

Methodologically, 'critical realism' generally looks for critical multiplism which is elaborated triangulation. According to the paradigm of critical realism, it is essential that the 'findings' of an inquiry be based on 'triangulation' of as many sources -- of data, investigators, theories and methods, place and time -- as possible because of inherent human limitations of knowledge, limitations in detecting errors and overcoming biases.

## PARTICIPATORY INQUIRY AND POST-POSITIVISM

Participatory Rural Appraisal (PRA) is based on post-positivism to combine the strengths of 'constructivist' paradigm and that of 'critical realism'. From the constructivist paradigm, PRA type of inquiry seeks to understand human experience as it is lived and perceived by the participants, the context of the experience and an inter-disciplinary framework for analysis of the experience. Critical realism helps PRA in evaluating such analysis and correcting for errors and biases through multiple sources, methods, locations and other ways.

All paradigms are human constructions and hence subject to biases and errors. With postpositivism we recognize that any methodology is historically situated and it evolves over time. Our methodologies for inquiry and our standards for judging those methodologies are being continually revised by a process of mutual adjustment (Guba:1990).

### *The Principles Governing Questionnaire Survey and PRA*

The principles governing the methods are quite different. Conventional methods such as questionnaire survey primarily seek a general law which helps in explaining a special event under given conditions. Based on a conceptual framework, the general law operates within given conditions. The framework shows the relationship amongst different variables, magnitudes of which can be measured by collecting data and testing it empirically according to such criteria as objectivity, reliability, replicability and validity.

In case of a questionnaire survey we are essentially trying to know more about the universe either by deducing from a sample or by complete enumeration of the population in the universe. One is basically trying to find a general picture along certain lines which means a set of common questions are to be repeated in a questionnnaire and investigations carried out on that basis whether of a household or of an individual. Given the questions, the answers are stratified and classified into different groups (common clusters of responses are identified for classifying responses into different groups) to find out the patterns underlying those responses whether across time or across individuals, households and groups. The focus of survey is on identifying general trends and patterns.

As compared to the survey method, PRA is primarily for analysis of differences in local phenomena and processes. It is based on people's perceptions for analysis of complexities and heterogeneity underlying socio-economic systems and processes. The answers to 'averages' and set patterns can be found only when analysis of difference has been conducted.

### *The Principles of PRA*

The following gives an account of the principles guiding PRA. These principles help in improving the quality of participation, ensuring depth and breadth of information generated, the process involved and also provides a mechanism for evaluation.

#### (i) OPTIMAL IGNORANCE

In order to minimise cost and time, the principle of optimal ignorance is applied by investigators which means knowing what is worth knowing and knowing enough to serve the purpose and not knowing the rest or not trying to find out more. Associated with this is seeking appropriate imprecision or avoiding precision that is not necessary (Chambers: 1993).

#### (ii) SEEKING DIVERSITY

PRA is concerned more with analysis of difference rather than looking for representativeness of results or data collected. It is looking for diverse events, different processes and forces explaining various relationships in local communities.

(iii) OFFSETTING BIASES AND TRIANGULATING

PRA is essentially a methodology to offset biases of the questionnaire survey method. It aims at offsetting such biases by being relaxed and not rushing, listening and not lecturing, probing and not speeding indifferently and looking for participation of poor and other weaker sections of local communities (Chambers: 1993).

The process of triangulating is an important part of PRA. For any data generated it is essential to check the reliability and validity of the data by putting them to different tests. Triangulation is cross-checking the data in different ways. This is done through use of various methods and by using different ways to validate information. 'Triangulation' is adopted as a principle to improve trustworthiness of data. It involves conscious, non-random selection in different dimensions such as (a) team composition, (b) units of observation, (c) PRA techniques, (d) locations, (e) time and (f) sources.

(iv) LISTENING AND LEARNING, LEARNING RAPIDLY AND PROGRESSIVELY AND LEARNING THROUGH PARTICIPATION

Local communities have their experiences, their history and culture, their ideas, their priorities and preferences. Listening to local people helps in portraying their points of view which otherwise remain unknown. The amount of learning can increase progressively with participation of those who form the subject of enquiry. In this context, the principle of openness operates where an investigator facilitates an individual's discussion and views, in a natural setting, so as to interact from within. PRA is also based on the principle of communication. Communication is not only an instrument to cull out expressions, giving information but also an instrument of clarification of the importance of those expressions from the speaker (Streiffeler: 1991).

The above principles contribute towards different features of PRA which promote participation and learning. Some of such features are that learning is iterative, methods are innovative and interactive and the process of PRA remains informal so as to facilitate participation.

A questionnaire survey, in principle, is looking for uniformity, identifying patterns and/or discovering general laws in an universe with regard to a sample population where the output of the survey and its validity and reliability are of major importance. Whereas, PRA is based on principles which emphasise the process of learning and analysis of difference and also to evaluate its findings. In PRA, the process of learning is as important as the output emerging from the process.

*Are Objectives of Questionnaire Survey and PRA any Different ?*

Both the systems of inquiry under consideration, the questionnaire survey and PRA can be undertaken with various objectives in view. As far as data collection is concerned, questionnaire survey and PRA can have similar objectives in view. Some of the objectives are as given below:

* For generating data for immediate or future use
* For estimating trends and ascertaining conditions of the issues at hand
* For validation or cross-checking of data collected from other sources
* For learning about the impacts of earlier or on-going policies and programmes and to frame new ones
* To know people's perceptions and aspirations

In the initial stages, a PRA type of inquiry starts with probing, generation of information and data collection. Hence, PRA sessions are generally conducted with other objectives in view. There can be a mix of objectives to serve such as,

* for greater and better involvement of local communities in people's action through their perceptions, experiences and capabilities;
* for training, raising awareness and spread of participation through training of different categories of persons involved, in the development process, whether from the government, NGOs, villages, banks, donor agencies, research, extension etc.

*Evaluating Data*

The issue is to evaluate the trustworthiness of information collected by different methods. Any data collected is likely to have some errors. Proneness to different kinds of errors vary from method to method. A weak methodology is one which is prone to more errors. It is important to identify the errors since they affect any estimation made from the data set and the conclusions and recommendations made on the basis of those estimates (Katzer *et al.*: 1982).

*How Errors can Arise ?*

Errors can be of two kinds (i) Bias (which includes misunderstanding, misreading, lying, inventing answers, differential/prudent replies and others of similar kind) is a systematic error and (ii) noise is a kind of error which is unsystematic and random.

Error in data collection can be present in the form of bias which can have different sources. Bias in some form and for some reason is present in most data sets and there are several sources through which it can arise. It is a systematic error having an identifiable pattern and can be minimised in different ways. For factual questions, it is possible to check the respondent's answer against a reliable record. For questions about subjective phenomena such as opinions, feelings or perceptions there are not many direct ways to assess the accuracy of answers.

The sources of error giving rise to bias are:

(i) expectations of the researcher;
(ii) such expectation as communicated to people e.g., wording of a question or even the position of questions can affect answers;
(iii) age, profession, sex, religion, race, language, dress etc. of researcher;
(iv) behaviour of people and their characteristics;
(v) research plan and design;
(vi) selection of area, place, time and people e.g. setting of an interview; and
(vii) one event selected from a set of events whose results might change if other events are chosen

As regards biases (i) and (ii) clues given by a researcher can be such so as to have results in line with the expectations of the researcher. This can lead to creation of bias thus defeating the very objective of an investigation. One way in which a questionnaire survey can take care of this bias is to keep both people and investigators uninformed about the purpose of the study so that biases from both sides do not affect the study. However, it may happen that the efficiency of the investigator falls in cases in which the investigator remains uninformed about such purpose. In case of PRA, since people's perceptions play an important role, participation of people and their analysis can guard against the expectations of the researchers. Or alternatively, the researcher is supposed to learn from people's knowledge and views and is not expected to go with a pre-set mind and foregone conclusions.

Biases such as of category (iii) can originate through age, profession, sex and race of a researcher which can affect the respondents' answers. In case of a health survey directed towards ascertaining the percentage of women suffering from communicable diseases, respondents can either avoid male respondents or be reluctant to answer questions or give misleading answers. In case of bias arising through the profession of the researcher, it may be observed that each profession tends to carry its own bias and professional outlook of professionals depends on their training and experience. For instance, economists tend to see the economic aspects of rural problems while engineers are more concerned with the engineering aspects of a problem. It is difficult to find people who naturally have total perspective of a problem at hand.

In a PRA exercise, the different sources of bias through age, sex and race can be balanced by altering composition of team members and mixing people of different age, sex and race. Hence, there exists considerable scope to take care of such a bias.

Bias arising through behaviour of people is indicated in category (iv) above. Those people sensitive to the expectations of a researcher can knowingly guess them, e.g. through leading questions and cease to be their normal selves and move the analysis in line with the researcher's expectations. The framing of questions can be such that they are not neutral and the people are able to guess the expectations of the researcher. For a PRA type of exercise, one way to eliminate such a bias is by not asking leading and closed questions.

*Sophisticated Sample Design not Free From Bias*

With regard to bias associated with research plan and question-design it is important to point out that even with an efficient sample design and sophisticated analysis ambiguous questions can produce noncomparable answers, leading questions can produce biased answers and vague questions can lead to vague answers. Many survey reports on rural development have precise figures on hectares of land ploughed and planted with crops, litres of milk produced and calories consumed by people. They are precise figures collected through surveys based on questionnaires canvassed to rural peasants who are generally illiterate of decimal measures but can express their estimates of area, yield and consumption in terms of local measures. Local measures vary from region to region and their quantification in terms of decimal figures is likely to be erroneous. In such cases direct observation and other participatory methods can help in minimising errors.

In this context, selected problems posed through the data collected are:

* different sets of information obtained from different respondents are difficult to compare and aggregate;
* even for the same items, differences in wording and emphasis can make the answers not truly comparable; and
* the results of descriptive interviews need not lend themselves to statistical manipulations. Some problems would be related to management of data collected where problems of aggregation and comparison are required to be sorted out.

Bias (vi) is concerned with representativeness of results to larger groups of people, events or areas. This is what a sample survey tries to achieve on the basis of a sample size where the sample is chosen deliberately so as to ensure that the sample is representative. This is based on the law of causation and the law of uniformity of nature, where if you find certain attributes in some members/units of the population it is assumed that such attributes are likely to be present in others on account of such laws. However, PRA is concerned more with analysis of difference and is looking for events, processes and forces explaining such relationships.

Bias (vii) results from selecting one event from a complex inter-related set of events. This is prevalent more in questionnaire surveys on account of the questionnaire-design both in terms of fixed set of questions and exogenous designing which reduces the scope for respondents' views on causality of forces. Data collection through questionnaire survey method which focus on either one event or a collection of events, would tend to miss out much of the inter-relationship existing amongst events themselves. This can arise because of inherent limitations of the nature of questions in a questionnaire, most of which tend to be in the nature of closed or direct questions resulting in loss of information, important in explaining much of inter-relationships, if any. Comparatively, in a PRA, it is possible to analyse one event in the context of a set of events and have as much information as possible both on absoluteness and relativeness of the events. In a complex inter-relationship, one event can naturally lead to another event or a group of events which can lead to identification of some cause-effect relationship. Because of open-ended questions information on inter-relationship of events is easier to understand and appreciate.

Error can also be random and unsystematic. This is what is termed as 'noise' in data and can be caused by the same factors which cause bias in data. For instance, noise can be created by the differences amongst the people being studied. Events prior to interview, education, personal problems and traits are not controllable and they affect the quality of data in different ways. Even for the best methods some noise is bound to occur.

### *Criteria for Trustworthiness of Data*

The question is what data to accept and what to reject. How to reduce errors and to increase the trustworthiness of data. For this purpose, there can be two kinds of criteria which can be applied — the internal criteria and the external criteria. In simple terms, the external criteria consists of all that the data has to say and to compare it with what is already known about the areas to which the data relates. The internal criteria, on the other hand, is concerned about the adequacy of the process and method used for collection of data. Both criteria are important for the evaluation of the data collected (Katzer, Cook and Crouch:1982).

As far as the external criteria is concerned, not many methodologies have provision within them for a comparative evaluation of data already available on the subject. Much depends on the aptitude of the researcher to evaluate the data on the basis of studies available in that area. However, as far as PRA is concerned, secondary data review forms an important method through which background material is provided for a PRA exercise. In the context of PRA, a secondary data review can precede a PRA exercise. It is considered as one of the techniques to help in better understanding of the subject concerned.

With regard to internal criteria, in the conventional approach, one can estimate an average error term and examine the deviations of the actual observations from the average or the expected observation. Greater the deviations greater are the imperfections in the data for such deviations do not help in forming neat relationships amongst variables so as to explain a particular phenomenon. The parameters of the equation explaining the relationship would have low acceptibility in standard statistical terms and low explanatory power to explain that relationship.

### *Criteria used by Conventional Research*

Conventional research uses four criteria for evaluating data which are internal validity, external validity, reliability and objectivity. Internal validity is about the causal relationship between two variables and external validity is about causal relationships applying to other contexts/situations. The criterion of reliability is the extent to which repetition of the same instruments will yield similar instruments and objectivity is the extent to which multiple observers can agree on a phenomenon.

Gill (1993) writes "a perceived strength of questionnaire is that its output is highly amenable to the very powerful and rigorous techniques of modern statistical analysis". The questionnaire survey facilitates this by the following:

* focusing on mostly quantitative (at the expense of qualitative) measurement
* generating a relatively large number of individual interviews (in an effort to capture variation)
* aiming at standardisation of questions across the entire sample of respondents, which in turn leads to concentration on 'closed-ended' questions.

In this connection, measurability of data can be distinguished in terms of qualitative or quantitative data. It can be qualitative such as a 'yes' or a 'no' or a 'good' or a 'bad' or comparative data such as 'better' and 'worse'. The same, however, can be quantified by means of binary numbers such as '0' or '1'. Much depends on whether data are numerically measurable or quantifiable. In the context of PRA method, one can also distinguish between counting e.g., the number of household members in discrete numbers; measuring — for measuring purpose one can do the actual measurement or one can estimate or form approximate idea of an amount or quantity (e.g., to measure yield of a farm to correspond to the true yield); and comparing or quantifying differences or similarities/likes and dislikes in respect of different items.

Gill (1993) remarks that the rigour and accuracy of modern statistical analysis is nullified by the above limitations of the questionnaire as a data-gathering instrument. There is no way in which rigour in analysis can compensate for an unknown and unknowable degree of inaccuracy in the measurement of independent variables where the non-sampling errors arising from the operational environment in developing countries pose major constraints.

*Conventional Criteria and Trustworthiness of Participatory Inquiry*

Conventional criteria have limited relevance for evaluating participatory inquiry on account of the following reasons:

* Basic differences in paradigms of the two systems of inquiry
* Generation of both qualitative and quantitative data in a participatory inquiry
* Open questions lead to multiple responses and hence leave scope for considerable variations
* Outliers are also considered to be important in a participatory inquiry, they also need to be explained as much as the 'average' picture.

Paradigmatically, in the positivist school, we are applying conventional tests to questionnaire survey in order to ensure generalizations, patterns and universal relationships amongst variables based on pre-set hypotheses which are either accepted or rejected in the process. Such relationships under positivist paradigm can be quantified and tested. Those variables which cannot be quantified cannot be tested and are generally difficult to be included for scientific measurement and testing. Paradigmatically, in PRA, all actors have different perspectives and their knowledge and understanding are socially constructed. There are multiple perspectives on a problem situation and there are different ways of expressing one's views. As in case of PRA method, a standard way to test the trustworthiness of data is to apply 'triangulation'.

*What is Triangulation?*

Team composition is generally inter-disciplinary and can be constituted in such a manner so as to have the information generated from different perspectives. Teams can have persons from different disciplines, sex, culture and experience so that data emerging from PRA can be discussed within a team and with local people by a team to clarify issues and select issues for further probing. The units of observation can be changed in order to cross check the information gained. One also has the option of going for deeper probing if necessary. Different groups can be approached separately or in combination so as to arrive at views from different angles. Other sources of information such as secondary data sources can also be used to examine trustworthiness of PRA data. Different PRA methods can be used to test and verify a piece of information. For example, semi-structured interviews can be supplemented by farm maps, livelihood analysis and flow charts so as to check and cross-check the information obtained. For approaching any topic the methodological design should be such that the method fits well with the problem under consideration. When it is a study of features, trends, characteristics and conditions surrounding people, quantitative method such as survey can be of considerable use. However, PRA techniques which are exploratory and analytical prove to be useful when data required to be collected relate to conditions which are ever changing and never stationary and the causal processes involved in such conditions are dynamic.

*Other Criteria Suggested*

It is often said that participatory methods constitute inquiry which is indisciplined and sloppy and involve only subjective observations and are not amenable to rigour and accuracy. It is often pointed out that if information is changeable, locally valid, value-laden and entirely open to interpretation then how much of trustworthiness can the information have? There are a set of four questions which users of participatory methods attempt to answer in order to show the trustworthiness of their findings. These questions are related to the following:

* confidence about the 'truth' of the findings;
* applying these findings to other contexts and people;
* replication of these findings in similar situations; and,
* certainty about the findings being determined by the subjects of inquiry rather than the biases, motivations and perspectives of the investigators.

Pretty (1993) is of the view that alternative criteria are required to establish trustworthiness in participatory inquiry. These relate to credibility, transferability, dependability and confirmability. For example, application of participatory inquiry without triangulation of sources, techniques and investigators and participant checking of outputs will be considered as untrustworthy. The criteria listed in Pretty's (1993) paper are described below:

A framework for judging trustworthiness of data and findings can be worked out in the following ways:

* Prolonged and/or Intense Engagement Between the Various Actors in order to build trust and rapport
* Persistent and Parallel Observation for understanding a phenomenon and its context
* Triangulation applied so as to cross-check information and increase the range of different people's realities—multiple sources, methods, locations, time and investigators

* Analysis and Expression of Difference so that a wide range of different actors are involved in the analysis and their perspective and realities are represented as accurately as possible
* Negative Case Analysis - revising hypothesis until one hypotheses accounts for all known cases without exception
* Peer Checking involves periodical meeting with peers not directly involved in the inquiry process
* Participant Checking to test data, interpretations and conclusions with people with whom the original information was constructed
* Reports with Working Hypotheses, Contextual Descriptions and Visualisations - the participatory inquiry team sets out working hypotheses with detailed description of the context in which they were formulated
* Parallel Investigations and Team Communications with the same system of inquiry coming up with the same or similar findings
* Reflexive Journals—these are diaries kept by individuals on a daily basis to record a variety of information about themselves so as to help remember immediate reasons for methodological decisions and interpretations.
* Inquiry Audit conducted to establish the fairness of the representations by examining the process of inquiry and the end product.
* Impact on Stakeholders' Capacity to Know and Act so that not only should the inquiry lead to action but the report should prompt action on the part of the readers not directly involved.

Pretty's criteria given above are to some extent over-lapping and it is possible to group them broadly into internal and external criteria as given in Table 1.2.

Pretty's criteria, as given above, relate to process, understanding of the context, objectivity of output, multiple methods, revising learning process, recording, parallel investigations, inquiry audit and the like. All these help in reducing errors in the inquiry process.

### Concluding Remarks

Conventional tests are looking at an average or 'normal' picture and any deviations from the average would either be smoothened out by further averaging or by dropping observations which are considered to be abnormal or exceptional and have major deviations from the average or expected observation. In conventional tests, while estimating parameters for causal relationship, we can apply two standard criteria, the 't' test for judging the

**Table 1.2**

| Constituents | Evaluation | Criteria for Trustworthiness |
|---|---|---|
| | | *Internal Criteria* |
| | *Process* | |
| The subject of inquiry from Inside | | 1. Better rapport<br>2. Revising hypothesis<br>3. Analysis of difference<br>4. Observation for understanding of context |
| | *Process/Methods* | 5. Triangulation |
| | | *External Criteria* |
| The subject of inquiry from Outside | *Output, Process and Methods* | 6. Participant checking<br>7. Peer-group checking<br>8. Parallel Investigation<br>9. Inquiry audit<br>10. Subsequent action |

significance of the parameters and the 'R-Square' and 'R-bar-Square' tests for judging the explanatory power of the equation with the value of 'R-Square' between '0' and '1' which when close to '1' has better explanatory power. The greater are the deviations from the average, the greater are the chances of the average relationship being rejected both by the two standard criteria mentioned above.

Many aspects of any society's behaviour can be quantified whereas others can be expressed mainly in qualitative terms. For instance, while assessing the public distribution system so as to enable the vulnerable section of society to have access to food, the general yardstick used is data indicating offtake of foodgrains from ration shops which are retail outlets of the system. This data, does not however, capture the quality of food-grains distributed, the level of satisfaction of the poor or the nutritional level of the poor. If we use qualitative method it may be widely found that the quality of foodgrains supplied is not of an acceptable standard such as damped wheat or broken rice or does not have the required nutritional value.

In PRA, each view is important. However, this does not obstruct the analysis in terms of an average picture. One can always look for average relationship for specific purposes. The essence is that search for an average should not tend to supress the other relationships which may be equally important in understanding the whole gamut of relationships existing in a system. Hence, one should be aware of the missing relationships and links in the system so as to have a total understanding of the system.

## Summary

In this chapter, the two systems of inquiry, questionnaire survey and PRA have been defined, illustrated and compared in terms of their paradigmatic bases, principles, objectives and ways of evaluating data. One major conclusion from this chapter is that the two systems of inquiry are based on two strikingly different 'worldviews' which determine their paradigms, principles and trustworthiness of their respective output. The belief system underlying questionnaire survey is that there are universal laws operating in nature which are present in samples and are to be identified and the data validated on that basis. However, in our search for an average picture or relationship we should not tend to supress the other relationships which may be equally important in understanding the whole gamut of relationships existing in a system. It is important to appreciate such relationships from the perceptions of those who experience them and are an integral part of the system. In this context, we should be aware of the missing relationships and links in the system so as to attempt a total understanding of the system from different points of view. It is here that PRA being contextual and exploratory by nature, evokes people's perceptions and criteria and encourages multiplicity and diversity of views leading to people's action.

# 2

# RECENT FIELD EXPERIENCES IN PARALLEL USE OF TWO METHODS: A REVIEW

There has been a range of experience from the field on the use of PRA-type inquiry for data collection as compared to that of questionnaire survey. In this section, I have summarised those recent field reports which relate to experiences involving relatively large areas and reflect parallel use of questionnaire-survey and PRA-type inquiry or some combination of both. I have generally drawn on (i) those studies which have used either or both conventional survey and PRA-type method for data collection; (ii) those which show scale effect in use of PRA-type method; and (iii) those which use a combination of the two kinds of inquiry for data collection. I have made a comparative analysis of such studies on the bases of nature and objectives, size, process involved, techniques used, output, evaluation of data and lessons learnt.

**CASE 1 : Participatory Techniques in an Utilization Survey for 6544 households, An Application by ActionAid, Nepal (ActionAid, Nepal, 1992)**

PRA techniques were used by ActionAid for a carrying on a 100 per cent utilization survey in 9 Gaon Bikas Samiti (GBS) in Rural Development Area of Sindhupalchowk consisting of 6544 households. The aim was to assess the use of ideas, skills and assets by the community provided through the project and to monitor attainment of sectoral objectives as laid down by ActionAid.

**Objectives**

The objectives of the PRA type survey were as follows:

* to assess how far the ideas and assets which the community has

developed with ActionAid are being utilized and its impact on the community as perceived by the community;

* to increase the community's understanding and sense of responsibility for its own development so as to make planning and implementation more effective;
* to increase the understanding of the poorest people's problems and needs, and to focus on the poorest;
* to know how much, and why and why not, the ActionAid programme was benefiting and involving the poorest;
* to build a database of household profiles including demography and literacy.

## Design, Process and Techniques

For the PRA-type survey, a training programme was organised for 10 days to train 15 staff members who were to become the principal facilitators in the areas concerned. They in their turn trained the field teams to reorient them on objectives, techniques and procedures for utilisation survey. The survey team also had local teachers as members in addition to the staff from ActionAid. In each field team altogether about 15 people, comprising of 9 local people and 6 ActionAid field staff were involved. CDC members took responsibility for asking questions while local teachers recorded the information. The duration of the survey was for a week in which the first three days were spent on training and procedures in all Gaon Bikas Samiti followed by survey work for three days using PRA techniques. On the last day the survey teams came together to discuss their findings.

The survey used PRA techniques like village map, semi-structured interviews, seasonal analysis, time trend and preference ranking and included a set of guidelines for them. There were about 130 village maps showing all households in the Rural Development Area , Sindhupalchowk. A set of five maps were made - a village map showed households and separate maps were made for education, health, agriculture, income generation activities, community organisation and infrastructure. Information about service utilisation by each household was recorded with symbols on these maps.

The villagers gathered mostly in public places and discussion began with a few villagers who gradually increased in number and subsequently declined. These meetings would last up to 6 hours. The first step of the PRA team was to consult a list of development activities from the villagers as implemented in the village. With the list of implemented activities the second step was to facilitate the villagers to draw village maps on the ground using sticks, stones, chalk etc., for collecting information. As time was limited not much cross-checking of data could take place.

The guidelines for utilization survey and the information available were taken as references for tabulating and coding the information. After summarising the results, information gaps were identified which were filled through the process of analysis and discussion based on results of utilisation of services. This was a gap filling exercise carried out between report writing and survey period. The information from village maps were categorised into two, one, the basic information required and the other was the information common to all or collected by every team.

Processing and analysis of the collected data had three major stages. In the first stage, the findings were discussed and summarised by GBS on utilization of services by communities for identifying information gaps. This included the coverage and non-coverage of the ActionAid activities and helped teams to discuss further on the causes of such non-coverage. In the second stage, baseline profiles of households were built up on computer programme DBase III. In this stage, the information gaps were sent back to the teams to be filled up. Before that a workshop was organised with the principal facilitators to discuss the outcome of the survey and ways of gap filling with the community and sharing of information with them. The third stage was filling of subsequent gaps of information by teams and community. The teams corrected the errors and filled the gaps. This was followed by subsequent discussions of the results at several levels.

The survey exercise contributed towards participatory monitoring through meaningful data collection in terms of both content and approach. This was in addition to the benefits from the participatory process of involving the community, raising their awareness and learning from them. The data generated for services and their utilisation included the following:

demography
education:
- school attendance

health:
- access to drinking water
- use of curative health services
- use of pit latrines
- family planning acceptors
- immunization
- use of high yielding varieties
- use of chemical fertilizers

use of improved compost
kitchen garden and fruit trees
irrigation

income generation:
skill training and use of skills
income generation programme support
households earning cash

community organization:
savings groups
water users group
income generating groups

**Lessons Learnt and Issues Raised**

The problems encountered during the PRA utilisation survey have been documented precisely in the above study. They can be classified according to the stages of the work.

*Participation versus Universality*

There were some fundamental questions raised by the survey in terms of design. The survey could not be made more participatory because it was framed explicitly by the monitoring system of ActionAid where the impact indicators were designed by the system and claimed universality according to such design. The question to be resolved is how can the monitoring system and the indicators of a 'top down' approach fit with the participatory process of assessing them.

*Training of Teams*

In terms of execution there were a number of practical problems faced by the teams. One was that of inadequate training in PRA techniques, PRA being relatively new to the team members. Such short training in PRA techniques was not adequate enough to generate conceptual clarity on issues related to participation.

*Use of Guidelines as Questionnaire*

Sometimes, the utilisation survey guidelines (See Appendix 'A') were used by PRA team as structured questionnaires in filling of formats rather than use of village maps to fill them. There appears some scope for improvement in framing of questions and use of visual techniques for sharing of information with community members.

*Shortage of Time*

The utilisation survey had limited period of time allotted to it for its completion. The duration was that of a week which included field-work and training. The shortage of time hindered the survey from being conducted in an informal and relaxed manner.

*Open-endedness Leading to too much and too Little*

To avoid structured questions the survey started first with response of the villagers in order to determine what information was to be collected. This together with semi-structuring of questions created scope for the survey team to pick and choose the information to be collected. Although this helped in projecting villager's perceptions of developmental activities it resulted in collection of various pieces of information in different villages which were not parallel to one and another and hence were difficult to be matched. In some cases there was excessive information.

*Season*

It was realised by the PRA team that seasons had an important bearing on the kind of information collected. Some kinds of information could be collected only during appropriate seasons and it was suggested by the study that data collection for monitoring should include such dimension in its regular schedule.

*Data too Many and Disparate*

Data collected was diverse and not uniform and the recording of the team was not systematic. Lack of uniformity was due to inadequate planning in advance for the work undertaken and the survey fell into the trap of collecting too much of data. This was the result of prior emphasis on information relating to utilisation indicators than on analysis and management of such data. The study suggests that the process of analysing information should be left to the survey team. Because of their nearness to the original source of information they are in a better position to understand the symbols, legends, field notes, identify errors and also correct them.

**Further Issues**

* The ActionAid Nepal (1992) is an innovative study towards participatory monitoring and evaluation. There are many lessons to be learnt from the exercise in terms of training, design, process, analysis and output of PRA which have already been discussed above. In the study the process of checking data was very important. The critical component of the process was identification of gap in rechecking and processing of data and bringing them back to the village for correction and gap filling.
* One objective of the utilisation survey was the focus on involving and benefiting the poorest people in the villages and increasing their understanding of problems and needs. However, in the study, we do not find a discussion of the technique used to identify the poorest such as wealth ranking by community and the results thereby. Hence we assume that this objective although initially taken up was not pursued properly while the objectives of assessing utilisation of assets developed by the communities was in the forefront.
* The study has provided descriptive statistics on different services like access to drinking water, health, use of curative health services, use of pit latrines, immunisation, family planning, use of high yielding variety seeds, use of chemical fertilisers, use of improved compost, having kitchen gardens and fruit trees and others. The study does not provide any analysis of the reasons for high or low utilisation of services by the community. The study has not mentioned the factors determining the utilisation statistics. Any monitoring and evaluation survey would certainly benefit from the statistics projected by the study but would benefit further from an understanding the factors explaining such statistics so that mid-way corrections can be suggested into ActionAid's programme of community development.
* A range of PRA techniques have been used for the study but the scope for sequencing of such methods have not found preference with the PRA team. Such sequencing would have helped in moving from descriptive statistics as obtained from village maps to probing of such statistics using other techniques of PRA such as problem ranking in terms of the service or asset utilisation. In any case, the results of the utilisation survey, basically portraying its characteristics indicate that the scope for probing has not been fully appreciated so as to identify and

analyse the causes involved behind such characteristics. The study, however, is an innovative one in the area of participatory monitoring and evaluation.

**CASE 2 : Comparing Participatory Techniques with Questionnaires for Food Security Indicators, An Application by IFPRI-ICRISAT-APAU (Haddad *et al.*, 1993)**

Haddad *et al.* (1993), in a multidisciplinary, collaborative project, attempted to field test and document alternative indicators of food and nutrition security in the Indian semi-arid tropics. The IFPRI (International Food Policy Research Institute)-ICRISAT (International Crops Research Institute for the Semi-Arid Tropics)-APAU (Andhra Pradesh Agricultural University) project intended to make food and nutrition security systems more viable. Its objective was to identify 'alternative' indicators that can be used in food and nutrition monitoring and evaluation systems.

*Design, Process and Technique*

The project was conducted in four Indian villages formerly studied by ICRISAT. A week long training exercise was arranged through NGOs, Myrada and Outreach to train the investigators in PRA. The study villages were located in three districts in two states of India, namely Andhra Pradesh and Maharashtra. The study collected alternative indicators of individual household and village food security based on five approaches which were nutrition survey, economic survey, PRA techniques, ethnography and serum analysis. The outcomes of the five different approaches are being systematically compared where traditional indicators are important and the performance of the alternative indicators are being judged by their ability to track movements in the traditional indicators.

A total of 320 households were surveyed from four villages. The criteria for selection of households included those with children less than 18 years of age. The survey was conducted in rounds to represent both peak and lean periods of food production and labour demand and also a round of 'medium production and high morbidity'. In the survey modules, the form of alternative indicators were kept as simple as possible. For instance, instead of estimating income level, the number of income sources and interruptions in household income flows were recorded for each household. Due to financial constraint the nutrition and health questions were focused on females and children. Gender-related contrasts were performed for all age groups in two villages.

In addition to the survey data, the project team also collected data in two villages by PRA techniques for which four different PRA exercises were conducted concurrently with the survey work. The four exercises chosen for the study were village mapping, food charts, women's activity charts, and seasonality charts. Village mapping was used to identify households that were exposed to 'very high risk' and 'no risk' of food and nutrition as defined by the villagers. Essentially, the technique involved asking a group of villagers to draw a map of their village. Subsequently, a larger group of villagers was asked to identify those households which were in the category of 'very high risk'. This identification exercise was gender-based where men and women separately showed their perceptions of risk.

In case of food chart, the key participant in charge of food supply was asked to picture the food currently consumed by the household. The participant was asked to place 10 beans on the food most consumed and one bean on the top of the food item least consumed and other kinds of food ranked in relation to the number of beans in these two columns. Women's activity charts were similar to the food charts where the activities were ranked. The fourth PRA technique was the use of seasonality chart. This technique was conducted with small groups of different castes and gender to understand the monthly variations in rainfall, harvests of two main staples, food consumption, male and female labour demand, childhood illness, and women's illness over a period of 12 months. Once these charts were completed they were to be compared with the survey results. From the village map the 'emic' indicators of a household identified as 'at risk' by the villagers were to be constructed which could then be compared with the traditional 'etic' indicators derived from the survey.

An ethnographic study was also conducted by the project in two villages so as to learn how villagers interpret the terms of 'hunger' and food insecurity'. This was done during the duration of each survey round. In the serum analyses of the project, serum measurements of vitamin A and iron status were collected for pre-schoolers and their mothers so as to provide objective 'benchmarks' of micronutrient adequacy.

*Result*

The indicators generated from the household survey, the PRA exercise, and the ethnographic case studies may be classified into two broad categories: indicators that change values frequently (such as the number of unique food consumed) and those that do not (such as landholdings or quality of dwelling).

The cost of collecting and analysing different indicators is also being studied by the project by collecting detailed information on time spent in each activity, as well as the cost of supplies required for each method of data collection and data analysis. The performance of the alternative indicators will also be judged by their relative cost-effectiveness.

*Selected Issues in Haddad et al. (1993)*

The study has applied a variety of methods for a comparative evaluation of the situation under consideration. As far as the methods are concerned the study shows many innovative features. First of all, it is rarely seen that a study uses five methods so as to adopt different approaches in order to collect quantitative and qualitative data on the indicators of food security. Hence the study is interesting from that point of view. It provides an opportunity for a comparative evaluation of the methods in the field. In this study, PRA method is used to check survey results and PRA record forms have been devised for the PRA exercises which are different from questionnaires or schedules because they provide a set of guidelines for the PRA sessions and are flexible and open-ended. For example, the form on 'general comments on the mapping exercise' (See Appendix 'A') is a part of the record form where general elements and comments on mapping can be recorded by the investigator. The record form has details regarding recording of time, duration, name and others.

PRA-type inquiry as used in the project has demonstrated a fair amount of flexibility in the process adopted. It has ways to ensure that probing takes place and has specific allowance for more time, if required, which is documented in the record forms. There are some structured but open questions which are suppose to follow the 'visual' techniques in PRA and the emphasis is on as much disaggregation as possible so as to resist aggregation. For the project, not only are the 'visuals' important but analysis of them are equally important. The study applies a variety of PRA techniques thought as appropriate for the study, like mapping, food chart, seasonality and time activity chart. In the PRA sessions, the key informant is also the key performant (performing the activities) e.g., for the food charts, the key performant is usually the mother, the daughter-in-law or the grandmother. The analysis of difference via gender analysis is an integral part of the project. Cross checking is in-built into guidelines at each point whether through groups, investigators, methods, seasons, places, note taking or while moving from one 'visual' to another 'visual' technique of the same kind. The project has included cross-checking of PRA data by participants as well as by gender.

The study has much scope for improvement. Some of them are described below. The process of rapport building which takes place before the PRA data is generated also needs to be documented in the study for it is generally different with different groups of participants. Such process has its impact on the PRA output, whether small or large. As far as the study is concerned I do not find much emphasis on the process of rapport building. Again, the same set of PRA techniques are used by the investigators and the project does not leave much space to use other techniques and virtually there is no scope for any innovation by the participants. Scoring is fixed in terms of seeds and is being guided by the project. The flexibility of scoring in terms of 'free' or 'fixed' scoring has been lost. The sequencing of techniques, which can lead to their cumulative impact on the output has not been approached and this appears to be a lost opportunity for the project.

One structured element in the project is the direction of probing and a few suggested questions. There is no mention of what to do when things do not happen the way they should happen. No alternative ways are suggested to start the PRA exercises. Sometimes it appears from the guidelines that subtle structuring as given in record forms has prevented further probing into the theme. Sometimes the linkages are missing in the visual techniques of PRA in absence of 'sequencing of methods' and hence the questions asked on the 'visuals' are limited to that extent and are, in a way, preventing continuity of analysis by the participants. Other factors related to the theme, which require analysis through PRA exercises are the sources of food, ways to procure food, primary and secondary food security, expenditure on food in relation to income, accessibility to public distribution system and eating habits of wild food and their availability. We do not know as to what extent the year of the study is different from the previous years in terms of food insecurity. In short, the study has not made use of the PRA techniques to their full potential, however, it does provide a reasonable picture of what all is possible with the use of such techniques.

Another point which needs mention in this study is that PRA method is essentially geared to data collection in the area of food security/ insecurity and is extractive in that sense. It does not talk of people's priorities or actions in changing their quality of life. The emphasis being on the participants acting as objects of testing food security measures and not on what they are capable of doing in terms of community participation towards ensuring their own food security. Since the data collection has little or no provision regarding this aspect we are left thinking in what way the villagers can be involved in improving their own food security arrangements.

**CASE 3: Comparing Wealth Ranking by Participatory Rural Appraisal and Formal Surveys, Tamil Nadu, India: An Approach by RUHSA (Rajaratnam *et al.* : 1993)**

RUHSA has validated the method of wealth ranking by PRA *vs.* survey in identifying the rural poor. The utility of such a study, as stated by Rajaratnam *et al.* (1993), is for poverty alleviation programme where it is important to correctly identify the rural poor so as to effectively plan, implement and evaluate such programmes. The objectives of the study are:

* to identify the type of indicators used by the community to classify their economic status;
* to validate professionals' classification with community classification using wealth ranking technique of PRA; and
* to determine the reasons for wrong classification of certain households by community and by professionals.

*Design, Process and Technique*

The study was conducted in Maliapattu Panchayat of Tamil Nadu, India, which has 412 households residing in three different clusters. Both questionnaire survey and PRA method were used for the study. The four major steps in the study were:

* prioritisation of households initially by professionals and by community;
* matching the prioritisation of the two groups;
* verifying the differed priorities by both the methods under consideration; and,
* validation of prioritisation along with reasons for differences.

The first was a formal survey conducted by an experienced and trained team to assess the economic status of each household using a pretested structured schedule. Steps were taken to ensure validity of data while collecting, editing and computerising. Once the data were computerised and ready for analysis, different combinations of indicators were tried out to fix the economic level of each households. The selected indicators chosen by the investigators for professional classification were caste, type of roof, type of house, education, occupation, land, per capita income and average set of dresses.

The wealth ranking technique of PRA was applied at three places with two different groups of men and women, of minimum four informants, each, being interviewed at each place. The groups classified the households into poor, middle and rich by use of Grandin's method of card sorting. Each household was represented by a card which was sorted into piles by the informants according to their criteria.

As regards the validation of the classification of households by groups of local people the study proceeded in the following manner. Each household was classified on the basis of intense discussion and any difference of opinion was sorted out by further discussion. The reasons for classification were noted on a sheet. In order to have further cross-checking of data, this process was repeated with next group of informants which was different from the first group and where the results of the first group were validated and the differences sorted out.

*Results*

The results of both survey and PRA wealth ranking were matched using computer services and the percentage of households with same and differed priorities were also calculated. It was found that on an average, only 62 per cent of the professional's priorities for classifying house-holds coincided and matched with the priorities set by the community. This made for a difference of 38 per cent in the two priorities. An in-depth investigation was taken up for 50 per cent of the 38 per cent of those households which fell into the category of differed priorities of professionals and of community. Such further probing of various key informants and the households concerned and cross-checking them with PRA and survey results helped the investigators to finalise the actual economic level of the households in question.

On cross checking the data, the study concludes that for the area under consideration, the professionals through their fixed indicators were, on an average, 57 per cent accurate in identifying the economic levels of the households concerned, whereas, the community using the wealth ranking technique was, on an average, 96.7 per cent accurate in identifying the economic levels of the households.

The study also documents the reasons for wrong classification by the professionals:

* With regard to data collected by means of questionnaire survey, the community did not reveal facts on ownership of land, livestock, assets, income sources and actual income fearing that they may not get any benefit from the programmes.

* Sometimes, lapse on the part of those investigating led to missing of information on subsidiary occupation.
* The fixed indicators of the professionals such as tiled roof for the rich or good housing conditions for the rich were also applicable to other sections of the community. Some poor households also had such housing conditions and hence such fixed criteria for classification was proved wrong.
* Another problem was that the formal survey had the tendency to break bigger families into smaller nucleus family so as to fit the concept of a 'household'. The wealth ranking technique of PRA was able to pick up exact information about the family and the local people were able to identify the functional family.

The reasons for wrong classification by the community were due to biases of informants towards their relatives or their subjective feelings of sympathy towards sick people who were classified as poor although their children were in good jobs. However, as the results show, accuracy of information was higher when based on wealth ranking.

The study concludes that the wealth ranking technique of PRA method is a more trustworthy process as compared to a formal questionnaire survey in identifying rural poor. In this connection, the study also point out one necessary condition.

One, that the informants in a wealth ranking process should be permanent residents in their community for at least 15 to 20 years who have detailed knowledge about each household. Choice of informants plays a vital role in obtaining valid data in the wealth ranking process.

In case of PRA method, the programme implementors working for the community are directly involved in the field along with the local informants and that helps them to have a better understanding of the community. Whereas, professional's classification through a questionnaire-survey is dependant mostly on the enumerators who collect field data and fill questionnaires according to their understanding and efficiency.

*Further Issues*

RUHSA's study is surely an important evidence on wealth ranking as compared to formal questionnaire-survey and has much scope for further improvement. In terms of wealth ranking it can be further improved in design. In order to have a better coverage of 412 houses, both geographical and socio-economic, some initial sampling can be done of the three places chosen for doing the ranking. In the study, Rajaratnam *et al.* (1993) has not explained how the locations for PRA exercise were selected and how the three locations chosen provided adequate coverage to the large number of households under study. It is not only a question of simply generating indicators for wealth ranking but also a question of matching these indicators with the actual status of the households and grouping of households on that basis. In this context, Rajaratnam A., in a later communication, clarifies that the places selected for wealth ranking were in community building and on river bed where informants from different clusters did the ranking.

Wealth ranking can also be done visually through mapping and this helps in locating the households on the map and visually triangulating them with different community members. If villages are large the community may wish to start by drawing maps of different areas for complete coverage of the community households. Rajaratnam A., in a later communication, is of the opinion that such wealth mapping may not bring accurate and precise information.

RUHSA's study also describes that the informants have been approached in such a manner so that they provide a balanced picture and avoid giving biased opinions with ulterior motives. This constitutes an important part of the process. The study, however, does not explain how this was actually done in the field. In a later communication, Rajaratnam A. explains this with the investigators having ideal questions and taking extra care to let triangulation process proceed until a common understanding is reached.

According to the study, it uses secluded and quiet locations for wealth ranking without local persons watching or advising. This actually makes for a non-sampling bias in selection of informants by the investigators by deliberately incuding some and avoiding others and also possibly missing the opportunity for more and better information. Rajaratnam A., in a later communication, is of the opinion that wealth ranking requires high precision where selection of informants play a key role.

RUHSA's study, while describing investigator's facilitation to smoothen heated arguments amongst groups has actually promoted conflict resolution rather than a process of triangulation as pointed out by the study. Resolving conflict situation and cross-checking of data need not necessarily be the same. In this context, the study has remarked that differences arising in the opinions of the two groups were discussed and 'invariably' sorted out. This requires further validation from the point of view of alternate criteria because two groups in the same area can have different ways of classifying households and they need not be identical. Nor is it always possible to sort out the differences and make them look identical. Perhaps the study needs more evidence and clarification in this regard.

In the study, the differences arising between first and second groups were sorted out with the second group only and not referred back to the first group for re-checking and reconsideration. This made the bias of the participants in the first group pronounced as compared to the second group. The study also avoided triangulation of PRA results with other groups in the community besides the ones which were consulted. It is here that visual maps for wealth ranking and grouping would have been of much relevance for cross-checking with different groups in the community for errors and omissions. All said and done wealth ranking of 412 houses is not an easy job and RUHSA study offers important learning points in scaling up of wealth ranking.

**CASE 4 : Participatory Techniques to Assess Change in Health and Women's Lives by BRAC-ICDDR (Adams *et al.*, 1993)**

Adams *et al.* (1993) conducted an exploratory study to measure the impact of socio-economic development on health and women's lives and their potential relevance to the BRAC (Bangladesh Rural Advancement Committee) - ICDDR (International Centre for Diarrhoeal Disease Research), Bangladesh Joint Project in Matlab Thana in Bangladesh. In the areas of Matlab, the ICDDR, has very detailed longitudinal data on health and social variables. An attempt was made to explore the potential of participatory techniques for establishing a baseline for the BRAC programme, and for future comparisons with on-going monitoring surveys of the ICDDR, Bangladesh, based on questionnaire.

This study was carried out in two villages, Paboi and Mohonpur at Jamalpur, Bangladesh with two objectives:

* to assess the effectiveness of various participatory techniques as a means of collecting information and
* to identify indigenous indicators of health, wealth and women's status, and to investigate people's perceptions of changes in these indicators over time.

*Design, Process and Techniques*

Five days were spent in the two villages, followed by two days of analysis and writing-up. The techniques were:

* social and demographic mapping

* health and wealth pile-sort ranking,
* health service utilization matrix ranking,
* time line and focus group discussions,
* key informant interviews and
* life histories of individual women to investigate life cycle events, income sources, decision making in health and response to crisis events.

The study-design incorporated triangulation in different ways, one relating to different sources of information, two, relating to different techniques to be used and the third, was 'peer debriefing' sessions of the investigators in evenings so as to revise hypotheses to account for outliers or negative cases. The study also used participant checking to summarise and evaluate discussions.

The study assessed several PRA techniques as alternative to conventional household census in collection of baseline information on village infrastructure, household demography, kinship, education, wealth and health status. The study has indicated approximate duration for each technique. Social mapping took one hour to one and a quarter of an hour. It also created rapport in a group setting. Different areas of a village, generally consisting of 35 to 40 households were mapped at a time. Extensive social maps were made on the ground and transferred to paper after subsequent discussions.

The social map was followed by demographic information on each household for which cards were filled by key informant using different symbols like coloured dots for age, gender composition, marital status and children, school attendance, BRAC membership. On that basis, the average household size and other indicators were arrived at.

*Comparison of Gender Maps*

While comparing gender maps in Paboi, the number of households matched in maps done by both men and women, with the exception of one widowed household. recognised only by women. Whereas, in case of Mohonpur, the same household were identified in 90 per cent of the cases, excepting that men participants showed a widowed household overlooked by women whereas women participants recognised three widowed households overlooked by men. In case of the number of married adults the gender maps coincided in 88 to 92 per cent of cases. Discrepancies were explained through women citing more male members than were recalled by men. In case of number of children the divergence was 25 to 30 per cent of cases for children under 5 and 30 to 35 per cent of the cases for children above 6 years. This was due to different assessment of age in gender maps for different age groups.

Following demographic information, the villagers did health and wealth ranking in gender groups which took nearly 30 to 40 minutes. The participants decided on different categories of wealth and did the card sorting of households into those categories. The classification of house-holds was verified and each pile of households was interviewed to elicit commmon characteristics. There was relative consistency in gender ranking.

The health service utilisation matrix scoring had a duration of 30-40 minutes and was used to investigate perceived utilisation of health services. The participants used symbols for listing of various illness and health services and scored them in a matrix using 20 seeds in each cell to indicate the services used most frequently for each illness. While investigating the substantial divergences between male and female responses it was found that men were primary decision-makers in health while women's decision-making was restricted to minor illness.

Time line and focus group discussion about change took 40 to 50 minutes. Small groups of men and women were asked to recall significant events which had occurred within the past 10 years. Using the timeline as the basis of discussion, the group discussed changes in broad areas of livelihood, health and women's status.

Key informant interviews with BRAC field staff proved to be useful in terms of information and insights. The key informants identified a number of changes in health and women's status such as perceptible increase in mobility, independence, knowledge, awareness and confidence and a slight decrease in the rates of divorce and polygamy. These were attributed to institutional interventions of socio-economic nature by BRAC. All these qualities were qualified by different groups of women.

Life histories through individual interviews took 40 to 45 minutes for discussions on intra household relations, decision making and livelihood strategies. Such interviews on familiar subjects helped in building rapport and facilitating open discussions in private locations.

*Lessons Learnt*

Some conclusions and comments of the study are as follows:

* Location of group work was critical to the success of PRA-type inquiry. Shade, space and quiet locations were necessary for focused and open discussions amongst eligible participants.
* Active effort was required to limit participation to gender or

specific group and discourage any person from dominating the discussions.

* Initiation of wealth ranking exercise proved to be rather sensitive requiring lengthy explanation.
* Social and demographic mapping was useful for household location, sample selection and establishing rapport.
* Matrix ranking proved to be a technique of considerable use for investigation of knowledge and attitude on a range of issues from health service utilization, to nutrition beliefs, to people's view about disease etiology, women's status and others.
* Timeline was a useful way of having discussions with groups relating to occurrence of events in past years.
* Key informant interviews with BRAC field staff were an indispensable source of information regarding the constraints and barriers to implementation, inputs and field reality.
* Life histories provided an essential starting point for in-depth analysis of the lives of women.
* Given the remarkable consistency of indicators of wealth and health in all groups, the study suggested a composite measure of household well-being based on the following indicators:
  food security
  land ownership
  type and number of income sources
  ownership of agricultural equipment and livestock
  ownership and condition of homestead
  days off work due to illness amongst household members of productive age
  education

* As revealed by focus groups and individual interviews, indigenous indicators of women's status and their relative importance were participant-specific.
* Studies of the pathways revealing change in women's status took account of women's differential position in a household.
* In order to document changes in women's authority or status within the household, it was necessary to go beyond the assessment of decision making outcomes, and to develop in-depth methods sensitive to subtle variations in power relations, and bargaining dynamics throughout the decision-making process.
* The study also suggested observational studies within households

as well as detailed investigations of both crisis and routine decision-making processes.

*Further Issues*

* A variety of PRA techniques were applied by Adams *et al.* (1993) for investigation of health and women's status. One issue, which could have been investigated with matrix scoring was the scoring on problem prioritisation of women. By means of this method a list of problems would have emerged and their relative importance would have also surfaced. This would have then helped in relating the problems with women's status. Status is determined by a range of forces and a visual interaction of these forces by PRA techniques would have helped to identify individual forces and their influence. The study has not applied visual techniques in this context. On the other hand, it has used focus group discussions and individual interviews for ascertaining women's status.
* In health service utilisation matrix scoring, the kind of scoring was pre-determined and fixed scoring was done out of 20 seeds. Such scoring helped in relative weighting. However, in villages, it has often been observed that many villagers prefer free scoring to fixed scoring. The study has not mentioned about the problems faced in fixed scoring and whether it was equally applicable and understood in the local groups concerned.
* Triangulation helped in evaluation of data. However not much was expressed about the applicability of the results, whether the results were representative of the two villages under study and if so, how, especially the criteria for wealth and health ranking. This is important in the context of generalization of the results.
* The study points out about indigenous indicators of women's status and their relative importance which differ depending on who does the analysis. The study does not mention how such known participant's bias was reduced.
* In the study, it is said that given the remarkable consistency of indicators of wealth in all groups and the overlap between indigenous conceptions of health with definitions of wealth, a composite measure of household well being can be created. Any composite indicator hides more than it reveals. One may point out that such a generalised indicator needs to be checked for seasons, focus groups, localities, income groups, ethnic groups etc.

* As for wealth ranking, female groups in both villages identified four categories of wealth while men did three. The study, however, does not describe how the final groups of three categories of wealth were arrived and how the underlying differences were sorted out.

**CASE 5: Evolution of a Participatory Research Methodology in Punjab: Water, Sanitation, Environment and Development, (Zafar, 1993)**

Zafar (1993) made a study of the role and functioning of Water Committees (WCs) in the context of Northern Punjab and Azad Jammu and Kashmir to understand the factors that influence the selection and the functioning of WCs at the community level. The objective of the study was to understand the concept of knowledge sharing within the community and groups regarding the water sector, particularly the functioning of Water Committees and how does that impact on community level decision making. Sharing of knowledge can take place amongst different levels for instance, from the external agency to the village leaders and vice versa, from the village leaders to members of their groups and vice versa and at the household level amongst males and females.

*Design, Process and Techniques*

The research methodology was based on the principles of triangulation and participatory data collection. In a participatory process of data collection, the basic premise is to hand over the process of data collection to the community so that they decide 'what', 'when' and 'how' of such data collection. In the study, the data collection strategy was three-fold. The first stage was that of identifying the potential information sources within a community such as male groups, female groups and members of households. Each group had different knowledge base and perceptions. To cross-check such differences data was gathered from all three sources -- male groups, female groups and households.

The methods and tools used were as follows:

* Household questionnaire
* Three Dimensional Model Set
* Decision Making Process with Visuals
* Rating Matrix with a Three Scale Grid

*Lessons Learnt*

* Use of Three Dimensional Model set with the male groups was not

that effective since the groups did not actively identify themselves with such picture sets which were not directly relevant to them. Whereas, Rating Matrix was more interesting since the groups had an opportunity to analyse their current experience on the functioning of the water system.

* Use of visual projective materials with women groups made a positive contribution. Pictures which were familiar to them helped in their confidence building and encouraged them to give their views. It also helped the researcher to set pace with the groups.
* Use of Three-Dimensional Village Model was empowering for women groups in terms of information sharing, raising awareness and confidence building. For men groups such three-dimensional village model created less formal environment and resolved conflicts. Such activity, however, was time-consuming based on more of a question-answer session.
* There were information gaps on the decisions regarding project implementation -- the approval processes, time periods and lags involved and faults with Organization and Methods. Men and women had different pieces of information on such aspects thereby complementing each other. However, such information was inadequate.
* Participatory techniques also showed that evoking participation in Water Committees can be a way of re-entering the village level political process.
* In Punjab, the Water Committees were not popular since they were not community-based indigenous organisations.

*Further Issues*

* Both questionnaires and participatory techniques were used by the researchers for study of Water Committees. The research design, tools and techniques, however, left much scope for further participation. The techniques were fixed and decided by the researchers rather than offering the community a menu of participatory techniques. Some PRA techniques which could have helped in further probing are venn diagramming, systems diagramming and impact study. Venn diagramming would have thrown light on the socio-economic relationships/distances, social stratification and would have also shown how representative the Water Committee members were. Systems and impact diagramming

would have helped in analysing and identifying cause-effect relationships. Such 'visual' techniques would have identified scope for further analysis and decision making.

* The paper indicates the advantages of a participatory process of data collection where the community decides 'what', 'when' and 'how' of data collection. However, the study does not indicate such stages of data collection having reached by the results of the research undertaken.
* The study also does not describe the ways of approaching different groups for the process of rapport building and process of probing which are integral to any kind of participatory research. The different male and female groups and the extent of coverage of groups have also not been described by the study.
* For reliability of information the study has used three sources of information which are households, male and female groups. Other ways are equally important for reliability. These consist of using different techniques at different locations and at different times.
* Proposed action based on participatory research has also not been indicated in the study.

**CASE 6 : Evaluating the Impact of Commercialisation of Rural Dairy Sector: An Application of RRA/PRA Technique (National Council of Applied Economic Research, 1992)**

A study team of National Council of Applied Economic Research (NCAER) (1992) made their first attempt at using RRA/PRA method to focus on the rural dairy sector in Operation Flood areas of selected regions of India. Earlier, NCAER had done a cross-sectional sample survey in all Operation Flood areas which had generated a valuable data set. The RRA/PRA exercises were undertaken in some of the villages in the three regions studied earlier. They were topical PRA exercises on dairy coperative and milk economy of the regions under study.

*Design, Process and Techniques*

In the study by NCAER (1992), a large number of RRA/PRA techniques were used at the village level like mapping, transect walks, historical transects, timelines, group discussions and semi-structured interviews. However, these techniques could not be extended at the regional level due to the limited coverage in the number of RRA/PRAs undertaken at each of the three regions.

As far as the results were concerned the ratio estimators compared favourably with survey results like comparison of animal population by type of animals, sale of marketable surplus of milk to different agencies etc. However, with regard to behavioural responses to situations/changes which are relatively fast moving such as prices, milk productivity of animals, feeding patterns, costs etc., there were variations in the results of sample survey and RRA/PRA method although direction of both remained the same or at least could be reconciled by environmental factors.

The results of RRA/PRA were close to those of the earlier survey on some of the major parameters. The RRA/PRA study generated additional information which confirmed some of the linkages and behavioural patterns. The NCAER study concludes that RRA/PRA approach cannot substitute for sample surveys. However, the former can effectively complement and supplement the latter. In some situations RRA/PRA method may prove adequate depending on the objective at hand.

*Lessons Learnt*

Some of the conclusions of the NCAER study (1992) are as follows:

* RRA/PRA can be effectively employed for monitoring and evaluation of changes in variables under consideration along with their linkages;
* For quantification on a larger geographical level i.e., for regional/state/national level estimation of parameters, the number of RRAs/PRAs per region need to be substantially increased (so as to achieve representative character). This, might adversely affect time and cost involved in RRA/PRA, however, valuable information will also be generated in the process.
* The techniques of RRA/PRA require a good deal of experience on the part of researchers for effectiveness.

One conclusion of the study is that RRA/PRA can be integrated with the conventional surveys in such a manner that the quantitative (estimation) aspects are left to large scale sample survey and qualitative aspects are confined to RRA/PRA.

RRA/PRA method can be effective in guiding pilot study for proper planning and implementation of the main survey. According to the NCAER study (1992), RRA/PRA's suitability for national/state/regional level studies is doubtful due to its present character of village level applications which carry semblance of case studies. However, this limitation can be turned into strength by integrating it with the conventional survey for wider application.

**CASE 7: Comparative Study of Sample Survey and Participatory Rural Appraisal Techniques (NCAER, 1993)**

As a follow up to the PRA-type inquiry on the rural dairy sector this study aimed at examining the efficacy of complementing or substituting sample surveys with RRA/PRA method based on comparisons of results, reliability level of data sets, cost/time trade offs, quality of field workers, training component etc. The findings of the study are on the application of questionnaire survey and RRA/PRA method in an 'Evaluation of the National Programme on Improved *Chulha*'. According to the study RRA/PRA techniques are capable of providing reliable village level database. The overall conclusion of the study is in favour of blending possibilities of RRA/PRA with the conventional survey.

In order to concurrently evaluate RRA/PRA and the conventional survey, all conditions were kept same for the two methods such as sampling procedures, villages and timing of the study, while, the techniques of data collection, size of the sample and the type of field workers varied. The study had the following objectives amongst others:

* Evaluation of the National Programme on Improved *Chulha* (or stoves) (NPIC) in terms of fuel savings and reasons for its non-adoption
* Distribution of working, non-working and uncommissioned *chulhas*
* Assessment of socio-economic benefits of the programme
* Suggestion for modification of the design and programme structure for its sustenance
* Forecast for likely demand of firewood in future.

*Design, Process and Techniques*

The evaluation was based on primary data collected from 130,000 beneficiaries (IC users) and 3000 non-users spread over 1600 villages all over India. For sample survey, the data were collected by trained enumerators in a pre-tested structured questionnaire canvassed for selected households. For conducting RRA/PRA exercises, the state of Maharashtra (India) was chosen and the objective was to apply RRA/PRA as widely as possible so as to achieve variations in agro-climatic conditions and socio-cultural conditions in order to have bearing on food and fuel consumption patterns conditioning the use of *chulhas* (or stoves). The process of sampling of the villages was as follows. After selecting districts based on homogenous groups of agro-climatic and socio-cultural factors, blocks were selected from which the villages were stratified and two villages per district were randomly selected. The methodological considerations of RRA/PRA type inquiry for villages was largely the same as sample surveys.

The techniques used in RRA/PRA were:

- social mapping
- resource mapping/ transect walks
- wealth (well being) ranking by card sorting
- preference ranking of fuel cooking devices
- semi-structured interviews of selected households
- group discussions with selected groups
- experiments on fuel consumption for cooking foodgrains along with semi-structured interviews.

The RRA/PRA team comprised of eight persons from which two teams of four persons each, were formed for field work for a month from mid-September to mid-October, 1992. The duration of PRA training of the field teams were for five days as compared to 10 days of training spent on sample survey.

In sample survey, each field worker was assigned, on an average, 75 respondents spread over 7 to 8 villages for canvassing household schedules/ questionnaires. In addition, village schedules were also canvassed. Normally, a field worker went alone to a selected village for data collection and contacted 10 households per village. Altogether 1200 households in 120 villages were covered in sample surveys for 80 days. For RRA/PRA, two teams of 4 including a local field worker, went around to cover all households in 10 villages for 30 days.

Some of the results were as follows:

- Sample survey was designed to collect data on several aspects of NPIC. Large sample surveys covering 120 villages generated ratio-estimates for selected variables which compared favourably to 10 villages covered by RRA/PRA. Some variables like fixed/portable ICs, agency/yearwise distribution/ mortality rates of ICs which formed focus of the sample survey were left out in RRA/PRA approaches due to the small size of the sample.
- At the village level, a comparison of demographic data through RRA/PRA and census methods revealed a variation of less than ±10 per cent which was much larger in case of village schedule data from the sample survey approach.

* RRA/PRA data aggregated at the village level compared well with overall regional patterns of households.

*Lessons Learnt*

* Training of field workers have a bearing on the quality and reliability of the information gathered during RRA/PRA.
* 'Learning by doing' facilitates complete understanding of the data collection process and enhances its quality in terms of accuracy and reliability in the RRA/PRA framework. Whereas, in a sample survey approach the training methods hardly contribute to enhancing reliability of data collected by reducing preponderance of non-sampling errors.
* It is difficult to arrive at a RRA/PRA based ratio-estimates for regional level estimation based on a few PRA exercises. As per the study the number of RRA/PRA exercises in villages within a region should be increased appreciably in order to generalise inferences.

Two major constraints as pointed out by the study were, one, to identify and train a sufficient number of field workers to grow into good RRA/PRA workers; and another was a serious limitation arising from the possibility of sampling errors in scaling up of RRA/PRA.

*Further Issues*

The study is of the view that the sample survey approach is geared towards regional level estimation whereas RRA/PRA is suitable for village level estimation. This is more of a presumption than actually proved in the study. The study points out that while comparing the results of the two methods it is possible to identify the tools that could be substituted so that complementarity/substitution of the one with the other becomes evident.

The study concludes that due to the small sample size under RRA/PRA approach a number of important variables were left out in the process. There exists scope for further probing of such a conclusion of the study by the following ways:

* increase the sample size
* focus on target population so as to design for inclusion of variables in question; if the districts and blocks are selected on the basis of IC

coverage then villages can also be selected on the same basis and not at random

* include not only non-probabilistic sampling of villages but also conduct further sampling of population and focus groups, user-target groups or spatial sampling of areas in villages
* target them in separate sample groups for additional applications of RRA/PRA method
* if too many variables are related then create space in the sample to explore such relationships
* test for quality of data of the agency which is implementing the programme under consideration.

It is only after considering the above points that a firm conclusion can be drawn on whether RRA/PRA leads to omission of important variables due to its small sample size. The NCAER study, however, does not leave enough ground for such a conclusion to be drawn.

## CASE 8: Participatory Questionnaires in Gujarat, An Application by Aga Khan Rural Support Programme (AKRSP) (Shah, 1993)

The note presents a discussion of some of the techniques "which could be critical in changing the mind set of the researcher from extractive to a participatory one" thus overcoming the problems of identifying and assessing rural realities and enhancing communication between the researcher and the respondent. These techniques initiate research through an open-ended process and are used for studying the impact of participation and village institutions on the livelihoods of people in Bharuch District in Gujarat, India. For an open-ended process, the two critical techniques used were impact diagramming and visual-interactive questionnaire. Impact diagramming helped people to indicate their perceptions of impact and indicators of change while visual-interactive questionnaire enabled people to participate in collection, analysis and cross-checking of information in collaboration with outsiders.

### *Design, Process and Techniques*

During the process, people participated in designing of questionnaire, developing their criteria and indicators, discussing important issues, collecting data and analysing them using verbal and visual techniques including questionnaire. Similarly impact diagramming, another participatory technique was used to indicate the impact of development activities. These included components like households, resources, livelihoods, environment, education, investments etc. These, with the help of group interactions were included in the checklist for interactions with individuals so as to enable the people to be involved in discussing and prioritising the relevant criteria before individual interactions were initiated. It helped in asking a range of questions during individual interactions and reduced question-fatigue. Additional aspects were added to the checklist with the progress of interactions on an individual basis.

In the note, Shah (1993) has discussed the evolving of a visually interactive questionnaire where issues described by people during group discussions and other interactions are collated and presented to groups in order to develop a common understanding of the issues. At this stage, the outsiders are free to add to the list after explaining reasons. People also develop symbols for different aspects of household profile and impact which are then used for information collection and analysis. Questionnaires on such a basis create scope for participants to exercise their choice of responding through open ended interviews and visual outputs.

*Results*

In Shah's study, the new techniques of visually interactive questionnaire and impact diagramming made for the following impact:

* It enabled village institution functionaries to facilitate the interviewing process and helped them in developing analytical abilities for future work.
* It enabled village institutions to create village-based information systems.
* Such output produced by villagers helped local institutions in their interface with external institutions in subsequent interactions.

*Further Issues*

Shah's (1993) note shows how questionnaires can be made more participatory and visual. However, one has also to think about organising such data and its management where each question-answer session of a household can differ from the rest. Shah is actually deriving a composite questionnaire from a preliminary interactive questionnaire. The issue is whether such an attempt is feasible given the scope for having unlimited patterns and degrees of response to such an interactive questionnaire. The framing of a composite questionnaire can become a complex task and highly skilled and motivated investigators are needed for achieving such a task. This, however, can be made operational with appropriate training in community participation and skill building. Organisation of such PRA data also warrants an appropriate design for preserving and maintaining such data base and also ensuring quick accessibility to the same.

**CASE 9 : Large Scale Wealth Ranking in West Pakistan: An Application by ActionAid, Pakistan (Malik and Edwards, 1993/1994)**

ActionAid, Pakistan is working in its first development area in Kalinger Union Council situated in the Hazara Division of the North West Frontier Province (NWFP). There are 11 villages in the Union Council with a population of approximately 38,000 to which wealth ranking technique of PRA was applied. The project has the following objectives:

* to discern and identify the causes of poverty in the area under consideration
* to understand which group of people are most affected by poverty
* to understand poverty as a series of interlinked social, economic, environment and political conditions.

In order to analyse the vulnerability of people in rural areas it is important to understand, in great depth, the dynamics between and within households.

*Design, Process and Techniques*

The wealth ranking exercise of ActionAid, Pakistan involved 20 people including field workers, people for planning and monitoring, consultants and others associated in data translation and entry. It constituted the following steps. Households in each village were divided into clusters of 20 where each cluster contained households which were located close to each other. Three informants were identified, both male and female belonging to those 20 households in each cluster. Baseline information of such households in each cluster was collected and the informants were asked to classify the households into different categories giving criteria and reasons for such classification. A programme was developed for processing the data collected. The computerisation of data is under process and the results are awaited.

*Results*

The output from the wealth ranking exercise were as follows:

* total number of households falling in different socio-economic categories and their criteria both village wise and in terms of the Union Council
* Baseline information relating to households and their different categories of wealth
* Report on several key indicators such as education, size of family, etc. in relation to households, villages and categories.

*Lessons Learnt*

ActionAid, Pakistan found the following advantages from the use of the wealth ranking technique. The technique is useful for understanding community's perception of poverty, the causes of poverty and the social factors influencing poverty and to create an awareness of the the causes and symptoms of poverty amongst informants. ActionAid also saw advantages in computerising the data from the wealth ranking process in terms of computerised integrated data base, retrieval on various key fields, updating facility, the program and its user-friendliness.

Amongst the problems and biases of the study ActionAid pointed out the following:

* Such large scale data collection exercise led to 'fatigue' for the PRA field team who found the exercise to be time consuming
* Sometimes the informants expressed their reluctance to categorise households
* The different biases posed a problem like informant's bias arising from those informants who were giving information about their own households, bias of those of the PRA team belonging to that area and the bias shown in recording of what the informants said
* There was also the bias in translating wealth ranking information into the forms for data entry
* There was also a problem of time faced by computer consultants because they were not familiar with this kind of work and had no understanding of the wealth ranking technique.

*Further Issues*

The study shows the application of wealth ranking on a large scale. The expected results of the study when finalised would help in explaining how the classification by different informants were different both within clusters and across clusters and how the categories were matched and how the data was cross checked with other people. One would also be interested in knowing what kind of an action plan is suggested based on the results of the wealth ranking exercise.

**CASE 10: Comparing RRA and Conventional Surveys in Local Forestry Knowledge of Sierra Leone, Edinburgh Centre for Tropical Forests (Inglis, 1991)**

The study set out to collect socio-economic and socio-ecological information by RRA which could be directly compared with the results of a formal questionnaire survey conducted by a social forestry project in Sierra Leone, West Africa. The RRA survey was conducted during July 1990 by a four person team consisting of a social forester, a demographer, a student and a community worker who was also a planner. The RRA survey, while not conclusively proving that RRA is more accurate than conventional survey, clearly demonstrated that an RRA-type inquiry was more efficient than the standard formal questionnaire.

The objectives of the study were as follows:

* comparing the RRA results to those of statistical survey
* to provide accurate information regarding fuelwood marketing structure and species preference variation in selected locations. Such information was required by the project to devise an appropriate strategy for marketing mangrove and acacia fuelwood.

*Design, Process and Techniques*

A FAO conventional survey was carried out by 6-project staff during a 6-week period in March and April 1990.

As for the RRA, there was a training period of four days in Sussex village, Sierra Leone, during the first week of July. The RRA techniques were used on an experimental basis to create a full socio-economic and socio-ecological fuelwood profile for the village. The techniques were applied in field situation which created confidence for the final exercise. It was a 3-week period during which a RRA survey was conducted in 2 villages (Sussex and Moyeimi), 4 small towns (Fogbo, Lower Allen Town, Newton and Songo), 2 large towns (Goderich and Tombo) and the capital city, Freetown. Five of these locations (Fogbo, Moyeimi, Newton, Songo and Tombo) were selected because they were part of the FAO conventional questionnaire survey.

At least three members were available from the RRA team on most occasions. In the case of availability of all four members the team would spilt into two pairs and either cover the same subject in different locations or cover different subjects for the same location or groups. The latter helped in triangulation of data. The team used the following techniques of RRA.

* Interviews
* Key informant interviews
* Mapping
* Preference pair ranking
* Indicator identification
* Fuelwood measurement
* Direct observation

The items for gathering specific information were as follows:

* drawing pair ranking matrices and recording pair preference results
* measuring and weighing fuelwood
* recording rough transcripts and key points of interviews
* conducting interviews
* identifying and recording fuelwood type and species
* drawing maps/plans of the research station
* prompting the interviewer if necessary
* noting species preference criteria
* checking for inclusion of all groups
* carrying equipment and supplies.

The pair ranking matrix technique created scope for people to be analytical in their species preferences. However, repetition of the technique for five to six times a day became tedious and was shortened by using three common indicators to generate the criteria and the ranking order. This technique was not applicable to the urban centre, Freetown, due to its low level of species knowledge.

The visual diagrams were simple to use and were amended in the field which effectively synthesised a large amount of information into a form that was simpler to understand and verifiable by the local people.

The research biases of the conventional survey were recognised and the RRA was adjusted to overcome them in the following manner:

* *Main road bias* : For overcoming this bias a rough map of the location was drawn on the basis of which the team took care of the geographical gaps and group biases, if any.
* *Local knowledge bias*: In order to avoid local knowledge bias the respondents were randomly selected and any opportunity for interviewing the local people was used. This helped in reducing the the time for finding respondents.
* *Seasonal bias*: In order to take care of the seasonal bias, the seasonal factors relating to fuelwood trading, cutting and buying were discussed during interviews. Seasonal calendars were used but were found to be too complicated and it was difficult to assess the impact of the seasonal factors. At times when it rained the team interviewed people while seeking shelter.
* *Previous reading bias*: The bias of reading research papers for conducting the survey was to be overcome by better learning from field experience.

*Lessons Learnt*

The results of the conventional questionnaire survey and the RRA regarding preferred species and ranking of locations were at variance for all five locations and a wide discrepancy in the results for Tombo. For instance, the conventional survey for Moyeimi showed that 66 per cent of respondents have no species preference whilst the RRA survey showed a high preference level for several farmwood species where every respondent expressed them as preference species.

It was not altogether impossible that the RRA results were wrong and misleading but it was highly probable that the differences in information on preferred species resulted from the inflexible and limited nature of the questions in the questionnaire concerned. The inflexibility of the questionnaire was due to the rigid choice of answer from a pre-determined set of answers designed in the questionnaire. The printed list of species could not be adapted to suit local variations.

It was not easy to correct the omissions and inaccuracies in the questionnaire by statistical manipulations of the results which were in the form of figures. Whereas, if RRA results were presumed to be wrong they could be corrected by project staff by talking to different groups of people. A point raised by the study was that not all of the 278 questions in the questionnaire were relevant. Hence considerable amount of information generated was superfluous. The emphasis in the questionnaire was on numbers rather than the reasons behind them and this again proved to be a hindrance to deeper analysis.

Part of the information gathered through the conventional survey was misleading and inaccurate in the context of of Tombo and Songo and hence unusable for good decision making. The questionnaire report also had a time lag of 6 months as compared to RRA results which were presented in four day's time. The RRA study also made attempts to overcome research biases generally associated with the conventional survey. The RRA study also indicated the qualitative factors to be accounted for while planning for fuelwood marketing strategy rather than the specific figures and proportions.

### *Further Issues*

The study by Inglis (1991) limited the scope of pair ranking matrix technique by using three common indicators to generate the criteria and ranking order. Averaging the criteria and taking the common three restricted the scope of ranking and lost important information in the process. The visual maps were also improvised and amended by the outsiders so as to synthesize a large amount of information in a simple form. The novelty of visual techniques was lost in the process.

The objective of the RRA survey was extractive in nature. It was basically for comparison of RRA with conventional survey and also for adopting an appropriate strategy for marketing of fuelwood. The involvement of local people in RRA was of a limited nature which was basically for data collection rather than their involvement for decision making concerning fuelwood marketing. Although the study took care of all groups, the tendency was to have an uniform application of techniques in all places for all groups. The flexibility to conduct topical RRAs and to arrive at results of similar nature by use of various RRA techniques were overlooked by the study in its attempt to apply the same techniques for all groups. The study, however, reflects important learning points while comparing RRAs with questionnaire survey.

**CASE 11: Food Security and RRA in Chad, (Buchanan Smith *et al.*, 1993)**

The paper describes an informal survey in Chad, using RRA techniques for understanding how people perceive and prioritise their food security problems. Such survey was conducted with FAO assistance for the development of a National Security Programme in Chad. The survey design and methodology for the exercise drew on experience of food security surveys carried out at a sub-national level in Darfur and Sudan. The survey was conducted between June and September 1991.

The approach to food security planning was formulated based on three concepts: (i) the availability of staple food; (ii) the stability of supply of staple food; and (iii) access of consumers to staple food. The survey had the objective of finding out at the grassroot level, how people perceive their food security problems in their daily lives and the solutions they seek. The final output of such exercise was expected to provide a range of alternatives and costs and strategies to achieve food security, from which national government could select its own policy options.

*Design, Process and Techniques*

An informal survey approach had very good reasons to be conducted. Some reasons for conducting it were (i) to make the survey participative; (ii) to conduct it in a short period of time with limited resources and 13 enumerators and (iii) to gather mainly qualitative results. The enumerators were well trained in formal surveys. They were introduced to RRA/PRA techniques initially in classrooms where they drew the first draft of a checklist of questions. This was followed by training in villages with a larger number of enumerators, where the check-list of questions was modified. Many visual techniques of PRA were omitted due to lack of time. Mostly, the training was on the structured questionnaire to the semi-structured group interview, introducing ranking techniques.

There were fourteen prefectures in Chad to be included in the survey. Within each prefecture, the survey was designed according to the principal production systems in order to ensure general patterns of food security problems and solutions to be raised. The process at the local level started with identification of principal production systems in each prefecture with the help of local authorities on the basis of which a representative village was selected for each production system. The survey was conducted in each of such villages which were 55 in number.

The survey team spent an average of one day in each village and the technique of semi-structured interview was used, first with a group on the basis of a checklist of questions to ensure some degree of standardisation. This was followed by interviews at the household level to cross check the information gathered in groups. At the household level, the women were mostly talked to with the help of a female enumerator.

Topics for discussion ranged from demography, consumption pattern, health and water facilities and other issues relevant to food security. Towards the end of a session, villagers were asked to prioritise their problems relating to food security and also to explain their current coping strategies and to propose appropriate solutions. At the end of the village visit, the survey team regrouped for a 'brainstroming' session to discuss their findings which, however, were not presented back to the village.

The survey was also conducted in a large number of towns, where different urban groups were identified and interviewed individually as per checklist. This was followed by ranking exercise of food security problems and suggested solutions.

*Results*

The enumerators prepared 40 case studies of villages on the basis of a standardised format by assimilating and organising all the qualitative information collected during the interviews. The final analysis involved assimilation and organisation of materials from all such case studies in a form useful and coherent for national planning. To facilitate such a task the results were discussed with the enumerators so as not to lose any relevant knowledge or experience. The huge and unwieldy data was made systematic and reduced by using techniques to summarise information concisely and sometimes visually. Frequency tables of problems and solutions were summarised and averages made. The background information on rural economy, recent changes, food security status and coping strategies were documented.

*Lessons Learnt*

Some of the lessons learnt from the exercise were as follows:

* The local people should be consulted when formulating a national programme.
* With limited time and resources, a survey based on RRA/PRA approach can be carried out on a relatively large scale.
* Enumerator bias can influence some of the responses of the villagers for which training of enumerators should be of a longer duration and village-based.

* Conducting the survey during a drought year can bias the results towards short-term crisis problems.
* Coverage of pastoralists can be negligible because the time of the survey can coincide with their migration.
* To begin with analysis of qualitative information can be an enormous and unwieldy task which can then be summarised for final use.
* Villagers, if asked to prioritise food security problems during a single meeting can make for hurried and superficial answers at times.
* Similar results can emerge from villages in the same agro-ecological areas.
* When wealth ranking is not used to differentiate socio-economic groups in the villages learning remains incomplete about group priorities on food security problems.
* RRA/PRA techniques can start from the grass root workers instead of with the national level planners.
* The expertise of local development workers is always a challenge to realise.

The study recommends some follow up work to be done with more in-depth village level work in some of the sample villages. It also suggests that RRA/PRA techniques are refined further to suit topical needs such as that of food security.

*Further Issues*

The study on Chad is an application of RRA to a national level inquiry. It provides an illustration of a theme-based probing at the national level. Some more issues are described here:

* As pointed out by the study, the application of visual and diagrammatic techniques would have improved the quality of analysis.
* For selection of representative villages for the production system, the local people were not consulted and neither was such selection cross checked with other information sources.
* The results of the survey based on purposive sampling of villages are assumed to be trustworthy given the right choice of the villages. In case the villages are not really representative according to the villagers, the results may not be representative to

that extent.

* The study does not mention about any wild food habit of the villagers in its food security analysis. Wild food habits are generally prevalent in both normal and drought conditions.

The study is, however, an important contribution since it relates to application of RRA/PRA approach at the national level and on an important issue like food security.

## Another Study related to Participatory Inquiry

In this section, we review one study in the area of data collection which throws up methodological issues for discussion.

### *Sentinel Surveys on Health*

The UNICEF video on sentinel surveys in health provides an overview of such quick surveys as applied to the area of health. It is an attempt to combine short questionnaires with community-based dialogues. It shows that community-based dialogues, accompanied by careful physical measurements can be quick and effective in using the perspectives of communities in bringing about changes in the quality of community health. It is based on the proposition that practical advise on what needs to be changed must be tailored to suit local conditions.

Sentinel surveys can have two instruments, of which one, is the questionnaire and the other is an in-depth dialogue with focus groups, within communities. Such surveys can be applied in the area of education, water supply, urban and rural development. It is an informal kind of a survey in which one interacts with community members to analyse and learn, plan and avoid e.g., health risks for which informed action is provided by the survey. In the questionnaire sentinel survey, as described in the UNICEF video, the health survey team uses a short questionnaire and physical samples of blood, saliva and others are taken on that basis. The answers to the questionnaire are analysed and the samples are checked and the results are communicated to the community in a short space of time, say a day or so.

The following constitute some of the important steps in a sentinel survey as shown by the UNICEF video:

* analysing data which already exists e.g., data on the impact of immunisation
* using a short list of informal questionnaire for 5 to 10 minutes in which all households are interviewed by a health survey team. A

general set of questions can be typed at the side and answers taken in a notebook. The questionnaire can be programmed in a portable computer and carried to the community and the answers can be entered in the computer on the spot.

* Samples of blood, saliva etc. can be collected from the families visited for testing if any.
* This is followed by data processing and analysis of two types of data, one of which is numerical as gathered through the questionnaire and the other is of physical samples gathered from different families.

Numerical data are processed immediately to give results back to the community before the survey team leaves the area. The results of numerical data and samples are produced in the form of summary sheets and fed back to the community. The analysis of the sample is also done in the field to measure 'risk' factor of concerned diseases and are explained back to the community with suggested treatment. The results of the sentinel survey are shared with district, regional and national health authorities. The end point of such survey is not prescriptive but analytical and is meant at establishing a dialogue. Such surveys help in planning of impact, coverage and cost at the local level. They help to analyse, plan and avoid health risks of how and what can be done and how such process can be supported.

*Further Issues*

* The UNICEF video has considerable emphasis on data management right from the beginning which gears the survey machinery towards giving quick feedback to the community. This also implies that field workers need to be of good quality with proper training so as to be able to handle data systematically, analyse it and give quick feedbacks. Such quality-oriented field teams may not always be forthcoming.
* The sentinel surveys pre-supposes the magnitude and dimensions of the problem based on earlier surveys which form the basis for selection of areas and villages and focussing of target groups. The dimensions of sentinel survey are decided from the 'top' management responsible for decision making.
* It is in the nature of a one-off survey which can be repeated from time to time but does not indicate a plan to build up on its database and community monitoring of health.

* It is quick for numerical analysis and sample testing. However, sometimes, such quick approach may not be appropriate for many communities which require time to open up for providing the information needed.
* The sentinel survey does not indicate much of rapport-building with communities in question and hence misses an important dimension of community-based interactions and learning process.
* The sentinel surveys are different from PRA method, in the latter the community is initiated to list its problems, explain them, prioritise them and put them in a contextual linkage. In the case of PRA method, the emphasis is on the process of learning about the priorities and preferences of the communities while in the case of sentinal surveys, the emphasis is more on the product so as to arrive at a quick overview of health conditions through community dialogue.

*How Do the Studies Compare in Terms of PRA-Type Inquiry?*

In essence, the studies reviewed in this chapter have shown methodological evidence in use of PRA–type inquiry and some have also used it for comparison with questionnaire survey. In addition, Haddad's study (1993) also made parallel use of methods like ethnography and serum analysis. The above review of studies from the field provides a comparative picture on how different variants of PRA method have emerged with regard to their kind, process, objectives, approach, techniques and output. One lesson to be drawn in this regard is that the form and the approach of a PRA exercise can vary from one study to another and this imparts a considerable degree of flexibility to the study concerned. This, in turn, has its impact on the output generated through PRA exercises.

With regard to objectives in question there is wide variation from one study to another. For example, ActionAid, Nepal's study (1992) is a kind of monitoring and evaluative PRA with regard to the utilisation of its services by the communities involved, whereas, the study by Haddad *et al.* (1993) is geared towards developing and testing alternative indicators for locating food and nutrition insecure. The study by Adams et.al (1993) is an exploratory one on health, wealth and other social variables in selected communities. Rajaratnam *et al.* (1993) and ActionAid, Pakistan (1993-94) are looking for types of indicators used by community to classify their economic status (1993) whereas NCAER (1992 & 1993) is concurrently evaluating PRA-type inquiry and conventional survey amongst other programme objectives. It may be mentioned, that whatever be the objectives, the above studies use PRA-type inquiry or the conventional survey or a combination to collect baseline information in different areas of their interest.

Another important variable in the above studies is the size of coverage such as the community or the village where the PRA method was applied. ActionAid (1992) undertook a 100 per cent utilization survey in the Rural Development Area of Sindhupalchowk consisting of 6544 households. The village maps numbered 130 which had 35,414 people shown on 6,544 households. Haddad *et al.* (1993), on the other hand, collected data in four villages for the PRA exercises while Rajaratnam *et al.* (1993) and ActionAid, Pakistan (1993/94) did wealth ranking for 412 households and a population of 38, 000 respectively.

With regard to the process or approach adopted by the studies some like ActionAid, Nepal (1992) used school teachers for taking notes besides their staff as principal facilitators. In most of the cases reviewed above, the study areas for application of PRA method were not new. They were either the service areas of NGOs or those areas where the organisations had access on account of relatively long standing relationship and hence rapport-building with community was a much simpler task unlike new and unknown communities where rapport-building takes time to start with.

As regards training in PRA techniques, the studies reviewed above show different durations of such training involved. For example, ActionAid, Nepal (1992) trained fifteen principal facilitators for 10 days and the field staff were trained for three days only while NCAER (1993) had a PRA training programme of five days.

As regards application of PRA techniques, some studies limit their use to just one technique like Rajaratnam *et al.* (1993) and ActionAid, Pakistan (1994) used the technique of wealth ranking, whereas, Adams *et al.* (1993) used mapping, ranking, timeline, group discussions, interviews and life histories. ActionAid, Nepal (1993) used techniques like mapping, semi-structured interviews, seasonal analysis, time trend and preference ranking. There is an element of choice in the techniques which can be tailored to suit individual objectives of a study and its requirements.

As far as cross-checking of data is concerned ActionAid, Nepal (1992) was unable to use it extensively on account of shortage of time whereas, Haddad *et al.* (1993) incorporated validation of data in the PRA design itself and in each stage there was provision for cross-checking of information collected. Other studies like Rajaratnam *et al.* (1993) cross-checked the data through observation of the investigators apart from checking by participants.

**Summary**

The eleven case studies reviewed in this chapter together with a review of a video on sentinel survey present a comparative picture of PRA-type inquiry and conventional questionnaire survey as emerging from field situation. The case studies vary widely with regard to their size and their adaptation of PRA-type inquiry and not all of them have used questionnaire survey. The results show how greater flexibility can be induced in field situation by adopting PRA method for data collection and analysis of local people's criteria. Chapters 3 and 4 also draw on the case studies provided in this chapter so as to examine the emerging field profile, if any, of PRA-type inquiry as a complement/ substitute to conventional questionnaire survey.

# 3

# PRA-TYPE INQUIRY AS COMPLEMENT TO QUESTIONNAIRE SURVEY

As evident from the methodological experience described in Chapter 2, there are a number of studies from the field on single and parallel use of questionnaire survey and PRA method for conducting base line surveys or for creating database for planning, monitoring, evaluation and research. In addition, there have been several other studies comparing questionnaire survey with other forms of participatory inquiry similar to that of PRA. In recent literature some studies have termed the questionnaire survey differently as ground survey/macro survey/formal survey and the like. Whereas, forms of participatory inquiry have been referred to as PRA/micro survey/ intensive local study/informal survey/diagnostic survey/RRA. The studies from the field have highlighted different areas in the comparative analysis of the two methods under consideration and have come up with relative evaluation of their strengths and limitations.

I can trace two different profiles emerging from the above studies, one, is that of using PRA method as a complement to questionnaire survey and two, is that of using PRA method as an alternative to questionnaire survey.

In the following section, I examine the emerging profile of PRA method as a complement to questionnaire survey and see to what extent it is valid. The other profile of PRA method as an alternative to questionnaire survey will be discussed in the next chapter. Both the profiles have different issues pertaining to them which need to be discussed and sorted out. These are the issues which can be highlighted from the experince we have gathered from field studies. In the following section, the relevant issues for PRA method as a complement to questionnaire survey have been outlined and discussed.

**PRA Method as Complement to Questionnaire Survey**

While many studies have used the two methods simultaneously some studies have suggested PRA's role as complementing questionnaire survey. On the basis of the field experience as indicated in Chapter 2, it has been pointed out that the use of PRA method as a complement to questionnaire survey can be multiple and diverse as given below:

* to design questionnaires/to re-design them
* to determine bases for stratification and sampling
* for estimation of selected parameters
* to reduce non-sampling errors
* to clarify survey results
* to validate survey results

Let us have a look at some of the field studies which have advocated the use of PRA method as a complement to questionnaire survey.

NCAER Study

The studies by NCAER (1992, 1993), on the basis of their results point out that PRA methods are capable of providing reliable village level data base, amenable to generation of ratio-estimates at regional/state levels similar to sample surveys. The overall conclusions of the studies point out to blending possibilities of PRA and survey for achieving better results.

As regards the capability of PRA method, as an independent method of data collection, NCAER (1993) concludes that in situations requiring few variables, social mapping, well being ranking and preference ranking exercises emerge as reliable and appropriate tools for data collection at village level as compared to the use of village schedules and household listing proformas. However, the study is of the view that the present household listing procedure in sample surveys needs to be followed for collecting requisite information on many quantitative and qualitative variables.

According to the NCAER studies, the blending of the two methods opens up possibilities of three kinds:

* pruning questionnaire size
* restricting large sample size to estimation of a few parameters
* substantial reduction in non-sampling errors.

Blending of two approaches as suggested by NCAER (1993) calls for modifications in the following procedures.

* organisation of fieldwork
* samples selected for PRA
* recruitment and training of field workers
* analytical framework.

*Rajaratnam et al.(1993)*

In the study by Rajaratnam *et al.* (1993), the list of households gathered through formal survey was used for wealth ranking instead of using PRA methods of social mapping or Grandin's card sorting. This constituted RUHSA's complete and updated list of 22,000 households on the basis of a formal survey. Hence the blending possibilities of the two methods are once again illustrated.

*Haddad et al. (1993)*

Haddad *et al.* (1993) made simultaneous use of a combination of conventional survey and PRA together with ethnography and case studies. The complementary nature of the methods helped to generate both quantitative and qualitative information, helped comparison of 'emic' and 'etic' indicators of food and nutrition security and offered a procedure for determining such indicators. PRA indicators which were found potentially useful were incorporated by the study into the conventional survey.

*Hubert (1991)*

We also have instances where complementary use of the conventional method with participative/informal methods have created apparent confusion but have resulted later in mutual clarification and complementing each other. Hubert (1991) in his study used both formal (open-ended questions) and informal surveys based on semi-structured interviews and concluded that the results of the two surveys were not identical. Ways of evaluating the relative importance of each problem/constraint was quite different in the two methods pursued. In the case of formal survey, the farmers mentioned their three main problems spontaneously and separately which is little mentioned during the informal survey. Whereas, during informal survey, a high percentage of farmers voted for problems which corresponded to their wishes which were then presented in a meeting and the relative importance of these problems was estimated by a system of voting by 'raising hand'. According to Hubert (1991) both formal and informal survey are complementary when they clarify each other.

*Longhurst (1993)*

Longhurst in his paper based on Rapid Rural Appraisal techniques and the monitoring and evaluation of IFAD projects in Sudan discusses the general principles involved in integrating RRAs with formal surveys. He is of the view that RRAs can be used to generate both quantitative and qualitative data in conjunction with formal surveys and additional data sets that may be available. RRAs and formal surveys can be 'mixed' together to be of considerable use in rapid diagnostic assessments which allow random selection within purposive sampling of sites and questionnaires with some open-endedness.

From the above section, we may broadly conclude that both PRA and questionnaire survey can complement each other depending on the nature of inquiry. If the method in question is the conventional survey then use of PRA can help in different stages of such survey. At each stage of a formal survey, PRA is of assistance in making the learning process iterative and meaningful and clarifying issues so as to attain the objectives of the concerned study in a better manner.

## How PRA Method can be Complementary to Questionnaire Survey?

The two methods under discussion have different operational procedures. For example, a questionnaire-survey with a fixed set of questions is operationalised through field enumerators, whereas, a PRA exercise would normally involve a multi-disciplinary team where pre-set questions are discouraged. The following account presents selected aspects of questionnaire survey where applications of PRA in different stages/ways can make for an improved design of a questionnaire, better canvassing and higher quality of output.

*Appropriate Adoption*

The questionnaire design is often the worst executed stage of survey preparation. The inappropriate adoption of a model questionnaire designed for one purpose when used in an entirely different context generates major problems. For instance, the questionnaire which is widely available in developing countries is that recommended and used in the World Fertility Survey. Its success in its own field, with its verbatim questions and directions to field investigators, does not make it a model questionnaire appropriate for a household survey or an agricultural survey.

Gill (1993) offers a series of arguments as to why for a developing country the problems of design and deployment of a questionnaire-survey is similar to that of adopting inappropriate technology from a developed country. Some problems of questionnaire survey in developing countries have been neatly summed up by Gill (1993) in terms of the following:

* questionnaire being inefficient due to people in developing countries not appropriately trained in designing it;
* questionnaire normally written in another language and translated before or during the interview;
* respondents not familiar with rationale behind surveys;
* complex issues, sensitive information and long questionnaire;
* often little scope to check reliability of findings;
* one-shot, cross-sectional output of questionnaire makes it difficult for trend estimation;
* tendency to give answers respondent thinks are wanted;
* enumerators, mostly men have problems in interviewing women;
* respondents either not literate or not representative;
* not literate respondents cannot correct any mistakes or misunderstandings; and,
* enumerators have very different socio-economic backgrounds from respondents;

Gill points out that "questionnaire-based methods represent a barrier to communication between the literate enumerator and the non-literate respondent. These methods play to the former's strengths and latter's weaknesses and in so doing frustrate the basic purpose of the exercise by generating data that are frequently inaccurate and misleading."

It is here that PRA method can come to the rescue of questionnaire survey where pilot studies through PRA method can be undertaken for framing of a questionnaire and its field testing can also be complemented and supplemented with PRA method. This would help in identifying the gaps in language, content and direction of questionnaires to be used for undertaking any survey. For non-literate respondents visual techniques in PRA method can help in answering questions which otherwise remain ineffectively communicated through the usual questionnaires.

*Informalising Interview*

The aim of questionnaire survey is to attain uniformity in asking of questions and recording of answers. Researchers are required to design data collection procedures that other people as enumerators will carry out. Hence the researchers and the enumerators seek standardization of the interview process. Such formal interviews in rural areas are almost useless because the rural folks are not used to answering a large number of formal questions. Hence, such a method may not yield appropriate answers, whereas, informal interviewing can produce better results because of its flexibility and openness (Ziche: 1991).

PRA method can help in framing questionnaires on the basis of informal interviews which are semi-structured. Rapport building sessions in PRA method can reduce the formality involved in standardising the interview process. For better results Shah's (1993) experience brings home lessons of making questionnaires informal and visually interactive. Informal environments can help in revealing and maintaining natural flow of answers which otherwise tend to get blocked in artificial surroundings.

*Vocabulary Made Appropriate*

The vocabulary frequently used in a survey means little to the respondents, particularly when the surveys are undertaken in rural areas. The terms used by respondents, their interpretation by enumerators, the quality of field enumerators and the actual words used in the questionnaire can create scope for considerable discrepancies. Here again one can make use of PRA for incorporating appropriate local words or appropriate clarification for words used in questionnaires.

*Questions to Anticipate*

Questionnaires are based on the assumption that the questions framed for the survey are sufficient to collect the requisite information eg. of household consumption. Much depends on the design of such a questionnaire and the knowledge-base of the person/team designing and preparing it. For instance, in case of eliciting local perceptions on a local problem the scope of questionnaire is limited since all relevant questions cannot be anticipated even with prior field surveys. Much depends on the kind of problems at hand, the factors determining those problems and their inter-relationship, indicators used by different groups of local people to describe their problems, the relative importance of the indicators and how they compare and relate to one another. People's perceptions and insights may not be easily forthcoming with pre-set questions.

Beebe (1985), while defining informal survey/Rapid Rural appraisal took it as a starting point for understanding a local situation. The informal survey was carried out by multi-disciplinary team, lasting for at least four days but no more than three weeks. This was based on information collected in advance, direct observation and interviews because it was assumed that all relevant questions were not identifiable in advance.

PRA sessions in advance of survey, based on checklists can complement in framing of questionnaire for conducting a survey. Such PRA sessions can be topical if any particular topic is to be explored. In such sessions different dimensions of the topic and related issues are expected to emerge which can then be sorted and incorporated in a set of questions for making of a questionnaire.

*Information Required Relatively Easy to Determine*

The practicability of the questionnaire is determined by the answer to the fundamental question of 'What is the minimum information that we need to gather'. The need to keep a balance between 'how few questions will suffice' and 'how many questions can be asked' does not need any emphasis.

A fixed set of questions can inhibit portraying of reality. Hence, there is a tendency to overcome this limitation by having more questions. A glance at many questionnaires is sufficient to show that controls are seldom applied. The tendency is to play safe and to include as many items as may be useful and possible rather than run the risk of discovering too late, of exclusion of an important variable. The minimum list of questions necessary to achieve the objectives of the survey can be very substantial. For instance, a close examination of the World Fertility Individual Core Questionnaire (World Fertility Survey:1975 & 1977) would reveal that generally respondents may be required to answer approximately 100 questions.

For any survey, PRA sessions in advance can suggest the kind of questions, the importance of the questions and the number of questions which are necessary to include in a questionnaire survey. PRA sessions can help in selecting relevant ones from a set of questions to be asked. One principle of PRA which helps in generating appropriate information is that of optimal ignorance, where one tries to learn as much as is required to be learnt for the objective at hand.

*Reducing 'Fatigue' Factor to Improve Accuracy of Response*

The issue is whether a long questionnaire for Household Survey for instance, involving 100 questions can generate efficiency. It is not difficult to appreciate that the accuracy of response generally declines with the length of interview due to the 'fatigue' factor. The more formal the questionnaire, in the sense that the enumerator must stick to prescribed wording, the greater is the risk of fatigue setting in. The time limit for a normal interview sets a limit to the number of questions that can be included in a questionnaire. It must also be remembered the greater the depth of the questioning, the more the respondent will be required to contemplate deeply about his attitudes, or go deep into his memory, and therefore more limited becomes the questionnaire session. The length and the coverage of the questionnaire can be extensive in the midst of persisting doubts as to whether the quality of response over the entire interview will be good and uniformly so.

Cases involving long questionnaires for survey can improve the accuracy of response by including PRA sessions. Appropriate part of such questionnaires can be kept for responses through PRA sessions where the nature of information to be generated can be decided in advance and the normal setting and the natural flow of probing can help to overcome the questionnaire 'fatigue'.

*Response to Identical Questions can be Multi-Factor Determined*

It is essential that the respondent must understand the questions; the respondent must know the answers to the questions; and the respondents must be prepared to reveal correct answers. Suppose the questionnaire is that of estimating income of a household and the following common question is 'state current income' or something similar. The enumerator must first ensure that the respondent knows what is meant by income. That, it is family income will give rise to other questions like whether gifts are to be included in income, whether income is in kind rather than in cash and similar other issues. It is most likely that the definition the respondent will have in mind will be different from what the survey seeks to investigate; and there may be wide variations in the definitions adopted by different respondents and also the same respondents at different times, if the survey involves more than one interview.

PRA sessions can clarify issues and also check for the responses. Such sessions can lend enough flexibility to adapt local terminology and local perceptions to topics, dimensions of which vary across individuals, households, communities and regions. It can also help in cross-checking of responses once canvassing of a questionnaire has taken place.

*Analysis of Difference*

Coming to differential pictures a questionnaire survey might fail to present the analysis of difference. One of the ideas behind surveys is to give an average picture or a general trend whereas an intensive study of a local community can present analysis of difference based on local problems at hand which is a critical element in planning and decision making. A good illustration of such difference is provided by a study (Lanjouw & Stern: 1991) where it was found that in a village named Palanpur in India a person had both high income and low consumption and the difference resulted in savings. The villager was classified as 'modest' through one classification but as 'rich' in terms of another classification. The villager's consumption pattern were that of a poor man for he ate barely enough to survive which led to his classification as 'modest'. While, in another classification he was categorised as 'rich' in view of his relatively high income. A survey would have classified him as 'rich' if it had looked into his income whereas, he would have been considered as 'poor' if the survey had looked into his consumption. A survey, however, would have failed to identify the phenomenon explaining this discrepancy. Such factor was discovered by an intensive village study which indicated that the motivation behind that villager's high savings rate and low consumption was his desire to build a small temple. This exemplifies that an intensive village study, can identify those underlying mechanisms affecting the incidence and severity of poverty which can be concealed in large surveys.

*Complexities of Inter-Relationships Projected*

For study of complex inter-relationship amongst variables, conventional methods like questionnaire survey with its emphasis on numerical figures has the danger of being elementary and simplistic. It is difficult to anticipate all relevant questions for arriving at such inter-relationship. This can again be unwieldy and diverse in character. The variables determining the complex inter-relationship, their nature and intensity and their process of interaction may not be easily captured through questions to be answered in precise terms and in quantitative magnitudes. The models based on conceptual framework can include only a limited number of variables and conditions and hence, is limited in scope. It is not quite efficient in practice to project complex inter-relationship of variables, their variability and interactions.

For certain aspects of socio-economic change in rural areas measurement is a simple matter and there are no serious debates regarding ambiguity of issues or rapport-building with the villagers, for instance, data on availability of roads, its kinds, number of school buildings, hospitals etc. Large scale surveys can be designed to collect data on such aspects. They can map the direction and rate of change in terms of selected indicators. However, a survey by nature, is constrained to unravel factors and processes underlying these changes and their relationships (Vaidyanathan:1989). And it is at this point that we need to complement it with other methods.

*Degree of Accuracy can be Improved*

In a questionnaire survey, the respondent can be asked to answer a question that is impossible to answer accurately, either because the answer is not known to the respondent or too much is expected of the respondent's memory or the respondent is unwilling to answer. In a PRA session on health, the local women were not willing to disclose the frequency of their ailment when asked how many times did they fall sick. Their response was that they or their family members never fell ill. When they were approached for stating how many times did they visit the near-by primary health centre they described the frequency and also the reasons for the visit. Respondents may be reluctant to answer questions. A standard case of respondents unwilling to reveal the true answer is provided by questions pertaining to family planning measures in rural India by the women folk, particularly so where the investigator is a male and the respondents are women. Response to some questions may be difficult. For instance, it may be difficult to find appropriate answers from respondents in the rural areas about gross crop areas or average milk yields per head of cattle, or about net income from informal business, or weight of food consumed.

Direct response to questions would vary from place to place and indirect means of approaching such issues will have to be devised on the spot, otherwise the accuracy of response can be affected in the process and important piece of information missed.

*Group Interaction*

Questionnaire in a survey is generally meant to be canvassed on an individual basis. This misses the advantages of group interaction which brings together individual observations and views and also provides a way for peer group cross-checking as a part of group activity. In this regard a distinct merit of

PRA is in interaction with groups and communities based on topics as facilitated by the outsider. Questionnaire survey can enrich itself by means of such group interactions through PRA where group views can be solicited in addition to answers given by individual respondents. Such group views also help in evaluating results obtained from individual respondents.

Such group interactions with selected groups are also useful either as a self-contained means of collecting data or as a supplement to both quantitative and qualitative methods. Such data and insights would be less accessible without the interactions found in a group. Apart from quantitative data, group interactions combine merits of two important means of collecting qualitative data in social sciences namely the individual interviews and the participant observation (Morgan: 1988). They can be cheaper and involve less time. In case of conflict within group on controversial issues either individual interviews are adopted or PRA is used as a method of conflict resolution.

## Summary

In this chapter, I have mainly dealt with the issue of PRA as a complement to questionnaire survey. Based on different field experiences, I have also described different ways in which PRA can enrich the design, process, technique and output of questionnaire survey. On the other side, there are many elements which a PRA-type inquiry can borrow from conventional survey for purposes of data collection. These have been reviewed in Chapter 4 of this study.

# 4

# PRA-TYPE INQUIRY AS AN ALTERNATIVE TO QUESTIONNAIRE SURVEY

In this Chapter, I present an analysis of a PRA-type inquiry as an alternative to questionnaire survey for which I have identified selected issues for having a comparative picture. Chapter 2, provides an overview of the studies which have used participatory inquiry, especially PRA method, either as a combination or as an alternative to questionnaire survey whereas in Chapter 3, I reviewed the position of PRA-type inquiry as a complement to questionnaire survey.

In this Chapter, I examine the field experience gathered on the issues listed below so as to have a comparative evaluation of the two methods under consideration. This will also help in gauging the extent of progress made by PRA method towards becoming an alternative method and the areas in which further experience from field is required in this regard.

THE ISSUES

* Inputs such as Cost, Time and Training
* Scale of Inquiry and Representative/Samplesize
* Process and Flexibility
* 'Elements' of PRA Borrowed from Conventional Survey
* Methods, Depth (Dimensions)
* Output
* Utility
* Accuracy and Evaluation
* Ownership and Empowerment
* Learning

**Experience Regarding Inputs such as Cost, Time and Training**

In this context, Chambers (1991) writes that data collection in large questionnaire surveys can be a costly and a long exercise and much of the data collected can just lie idle without being used by anybody. It can be costly in terms of financial and human resources and the time spent on data collection, coding, taping, cleaning, tabulating and analysing. The speed in organising and making the data available can be slow and can defeat the very purpose of data collection. There can be inordinate delays in having results from a survey which can make the data grow old and quick upgradation of survey data is generally not possible. The feedback may be costly and time-consuming. Bardhan (1989) points out that in conventional survey there can be persistent loss of information in case of ambiguities in interpretation of terms and categories with over-lapping boundaries.

With respect to cost and time, it appears that much depends on what objectives are being pursued for questionnaire survey and PRA method. The more the information required at the micro level the more is the time required. The mode of operation and the techniques used also determine the time factor. Apart from this, the formal questionnaire, in practice, can take much more time for various operations involved before and after data collection. With this in the background let us take note of field experience in this regard.

For any institution which is planning to conduct a questionnaire survey or a PRA exercise the following are the considerations involved as shown in Table 4.1. As evident from the table, many elements of questionnaire survey e.g., items no., 2, 3, 4, 14, 15, and 16 are relatively more time consuming than those for conducting a PRA exercise. Hence, time and money spent on them are additional components of the former method. It is expected that the informal nature of PRA makes it quick, given the same area and the same purpose at hand.

With regard to inputs such as 'cost' and 'time' the two methods under comparison show different results. As shown in Table 4.1, it is important to appreciate that there are many factors which influence costs and time such as the size of the study involved, whether it is sampling or census, infrastructural support, process, techniques applied, cross-checking of data and analysis, documentation and reporting. Some studies have highlighted these aspects of the two methods under comparison.

**Table 4.1**

**Elements of Cost and Time: Questionnaire and PRA**

| | Questionnaire Survey | | PRA |
|---|---|---|---|
| 1. | Objectives to be pursued | 1. | Same consideration |
| 2 | Designing Questionnaire | 2. | Check-lists, if any |
| 3. | Pretesting Questionnaire | 3. | Not Necessary |
| 4. | Redesigning Questionnaire, if necessary | 4. | Not Necessary |
| 5. | Sampling in case of sample survey | 5. | Sampling, if necessary |
| 6. | Recruitment of enumerators | 6. | Team to be recruited, can include local people |
| 7. | Training of enumerators | 7. | Training of the team |
| 8. | Enumerators going to field for conducting survey | 8. | Team going to field for PRA |
| 9. | Size of area to be covered | 9. | Same consideration |
| 10. | Duration of Inquiry | 10. | Same consideration |
| 11. | Filling of questionnaire | 11. | Techniques applied |
| 12. | Materials used in the field | 12. | Same consideration |
| 13. | Transport & infrastructural facilities required | 13. | Same consideration |
| 14. | Interacting with individual for questionnaires | 14. | Interacting with groups/ individuals |
| 15. | Coding, taping, cleaning, tabulating and analysing and computerising it | 15. | Evaluating Data in the field and data-computerising, if required |
| 16. | Checking errors, proof-reading and write ups/ copying | 16. | Informal Report writing and dissemination |
| 17. | Formal release of data through publications | 17. | Not required but may be done |

## *Higher Cost for PRA Method*

**CASE 1**

On comparison of cost and time of PRA method and conventional survey the NCAER (1993) concludes that cost incurred for training of field staff and data collection (field work) for the sample survey-based study are higher by more than one half of the cost incurred in their PRA based data collection. However, the study also points out that the sample survey approach covered 120 villages as against 10 villages covered (with 100 per cent coverage) in PRA for the study concerned. The data collection cost per village in PRA-based study as estimated by NCAER was seven times more than that of sample survey. According to NCAER (1993) per unit cost of PRA is higher than sample survey and extended coverage of PRA will escalate cost enormously even if the number of PRAs are raised moderately. In this context it is important to remember that in PRA there was 100 percent coverage of 10 villages.

**CASE 2**

Haddad *et al.* (1993) points to the need for more investigators for PRA method such as 'activity director', 'data recorder', 'mob control' and 'someone to do the thinking'. This, initially sounds like cost is on the higher side. However, given the magnitude and size of data collection possible from a group at one place such a team may be economical in terms of cost and time as compared to canvassing of questionnaires to individual households.

*Lower Cost for PRA*

**CASE 1**

The study by Rajaratnam *et al.* (1993) on wealth ranking of 412 households in Tamil Nadu, India, has provided estimates for the comparison of cost (Rs. 7111 for the questionnaire survey, and Rs. 1011 for the PRA) and of time taken (776 person hours as against 96 person hours).

**CASE 2**

Hubert (1991) while comparing both formal and informal surveys states that the investment in labour and material is much higher for the formal survey. As per the results the formal survey required 5 to 7 times more working days as the informal surveys and the time needed to publish the results were 3 times longer for the formal survey. He explains the reasons in terms of differences between the two methodologies, one, relying on informal discussions with farmers who are met on the way, while the other depending on formal interviews of a sample of farmers and observations on their fields. The data emerging from formal surveys were then processed with the help of machines.

**Cost Considerations**

In the above cases, cost of PRA has been expressed in terms of per village data collection cost or the ratio of person hours to cost or in terms of aggregate cost. It is not easy to arrive at a relatively simple comparison of cost for the two methods. There are a host of factors to be considered in this regard which can influence both actual cost and imputed cost for undertaking conventional survey or PRA-type studies. Some of them are as follows :

* planning and design for data collection
* training in PRA or conventional survey whether 'in house' or 'external' and the scale of training
* size of the area to be covered both geographically and socially, and the number of units, say for instance, households to be included which would also determine the expenditure on distance and man hours
* mode of transport
* materials used in data collection
* number of investigators/enumerators
* duration of inquiry, methods, analysis and results
* system of data management
* system for dissemination of results

On the basis of field experience reviewed above, selected points may be observed on the dimensions of cost in PRA:

* We do not have enough cases showing different estimates of cost inolved in PRA studies. We need more evidence from the field to provide us with trends in relative cost of the two methods under study. At present this aspect of cost appears to be inconclusive and we need to await further estimates of cost to arrive from the field.
* Once we have the cost estimates and the relevant break-ups, each component of cost can be examined to find out ways in which PRA can be made more cost-effective.
* As for incurring training cost in PRA for any institution, one needs to explore the relative financial implications of having trainers from outside at different intervals as compared to building 'in house' training capabilities.
* In case of incurring higher cost per village for PRA in the first

round, it needs to be explored whether it is possible to reduce external presence to the minimum and let the local communities initiate and have their own PRA exercise on the issues concerned.
* The 'cost' element in PRA needs to be compared in terms of rounds and frequency of data collection. It may prove cheaper to update PRA data if left to local community members for organising such updates which can then be evaluated in different ways to check for their trustworthiness.
* The aspect of cost for PRA needs to be judged in relation to its utility. One can ask relevant questions in this regard such as how and for whom the data is to be used ? what kind of data is required and when is it to be used? Answers to such questions can form a basis for judging the levels and increments in cost.
* If a part of the same machinery which is associated with conventional survey can be trained for data collection in PRA the overhead cost would be relatively lower than that of creating a new machinery for data collection by application of PRA method.

*Time Taken*

Next consideration for the two methods is that of time involved. The relevant considerations in this regard are as follows:

* Training time
* Time taken for conducting PRA method
* Time required for the kind and size of data to be collected
* Time taken for cross-checking of data
* Time required for data management
* Time taken for dissemination of data

The steps in conducting PRA method which influence time and duration are noted below:

* kind of data required
* rapport bulding
* techniques, whether 'visual' or 'verbal' or a combination
* probing on various issues
* copying of 'visual' output on paper
* taking of notes

* cross-checking of data

A factor to be considered in this regard is that in case of coverage for larger areas it is possible for the PRA method to collect data at a single place through group interaction. In this way, time is saved in moving from one place to another for collecting information. In case of participatory census mapping, data is generated with the completion of such mapping and is readily available at one location as compared to conventional census listing of households where data is collected from door to door and is available only after its formal processing and publication with a minimum lag ranging from a year's time.

Let us look for some experience from field on the aspect of time.

**CASE 1**

Action Aid, Nepal (1992) has described the time taken for training and conducting the survey and analysing the results. The training was conducted in two stages with the training of 15 staff members as principal facilitators for 10 days to start with followed by training of field staff for three days. Such short training inputs on PRA have been considered inadequate for the job involved because it does not provide enough conceptual clarity on issues related to participation. However, the study has not mentioned as to what length of training should have been appropriate.

The duration of the PRA utilisation survey by ActionAid, Nepal (1992) was for three days and the time for data gathering with the villagers took six hours in some places. A wealth of data was generated within such a short period of time and was considered adequate enough to meet the objectives of the study.

**CASE 2**

Adams *et al.* (1993) have described the time spent on PRA exercises and individual techniques. They spent a total duration of seven days, of which five days were spent in data collection and 2 days in analysis and writing up. The time taken for techniques are listed below:

* Social mapping (1 to 1¼ hour)
* Household demography (30 to 40 minutes)
* Pile sort wealth and health ranking (30 to 40 minutes)
* Health service utilisation matrix ranking (30 to 40 minutes)

* Time line and focus group discussion about change (40 to 50 minutes).

**CASE 3**

Inglis (1991) writes that RRA collected information in far shorter time using fewer resources as compared to 278 questions in a questionnaire which took six weeks.

**CASE 4**

Hubert (1991) observes that as per his results, the formal survey required 5 to 7 times more working days as the informal survey and the time needed to publish the results were 3 times longer for the formal survey.

**CASE 5**

NCAER (1993), in their comparative study on PRA method and questionnaire survey covered 1200 households in 120 villages in conventional survey for 80 days and entire households in 10 villages in PRA for 30 days. The coverage per village per day was higher in conventional survey but in terms of average figures it was an average of 10 households per village in the survey which was much lower as compared to complete coverage of households undertaken for PRA.

The above evidence weighs in favour of less time required for applying PRA method than that of the conventional survey. On balance, we may conclude that, by and large, PRA method takes relatively less time, interacts with groups and creates a range of ouput at one go. This is advantageous as compared to generation of data through the questionnaire survey method where such multiplier impact is generally absent.

On the basis of the above analysis regarding the issue of 'cost' and 'time' in the methods under comparison, I can identify two directions in the context of PRA method as an alternative to questionnaire survey:

* If PRA method has similar cost estimates as questionnaire survey but enables quick results then on most occasions we need to examine PRA method in the context of other dimensions such as representativeness, nature of output and its reliability.
* Alternatively, if PRA method has much higher cost estimates

in scaling up as compared to the conventional survey we need to look for substantial benefits from using PRA method in order to justify such high cost in using such a method. These two concerns initiate further discussions in this direction. This brings us to an important issue relating to the scale of inquiry and representativeness.

## Scale of Inquiry and Representativeness/ Sample Size

If PRA method is an alternative method to questionnaire survey then apart from considerations of 'cost' and 'time', the size of inquiry becomes an important consideration. The relevant issue in this direction is the scale of data collection. The question is regarding the possiblity of PRA method to scale up its operations and provide results which are representative of larger areas, say a region or a country. On this account, we have evidence, some of which are indicated below:

### CASE 1

The study by Haddad *et al.* (1993) relates to four villages of 320 households selected for conventional survey, whereas, PRA data was collected in two villages out of four villages through four different exercises. By the mapping exercise, the coverage of households in the villages was 100 per cent and general results were deduced on the basis of PRA data gathered in the two sample villages.

### CASE 2

Rajaratnam *et al's* study (1993) relates to application of wealth ranking to 412 households residing in three clusters in Maliapattu Panchayat of Tamil Nadu, India.

### CASE 3

The study by ActionAid, Nepal (1992) relates to a 100 per cent utilisation survey through PRA in nine Gaon Bikas Samitis in Rural Development Area of Sindhupalchowk, Nepal consisting of 6544 households. The time taken for conducting the actual survey was three days only and one of the PRA exercises was that of drawing village maps which were 130 in number covering all households in the area.

**CASE 4**

ActionAid, Pakistan, (Malik and Edward: 1994) covered an area of 11 villages in Kalinger Union Council, Pakistan, with a population of 38, 000 to apply the method of wealth ranking in PRA. For purpose of wealth ranking total households in each village were divided into clusters of 20.

## Scale Considerations

From the above evidence we find, that studies on PRA method involving large scale of inquiry are slowly emerging. PRA method is being applied across a large number of households and villages and the number of villages or households is not being perceived to be a limitation by the studies concerned in multiplying its results from PRA method. The present series of field studies indicate that the character of PRA method as a local level intensive study is undergoing a remarkable change in terms of application to larger scale of inquiry. The field studies mentioned above show by their results that PRA can be applied to larger scale of inquiry as much as to village level intensive local studies and it is possible to scale up applications of PRA for large areas under consideration. However, we are still awaiting cases of country-level applications of PRA and more studies are required on application of PRA method to large regions and at the country level.

We are aware of the possibility of large scale inquiry through PRA but are unable to conclude on PRA applications at the country level because we do not have enough supportive material at present. The scope for appropriate field evidence is limited in this direction because the spread of PRA is mostly amongst local NGOs who are applying it on a relatively smaller scale. The official data collection machinery is yet to experiment with PRA's capabilities. Unless such machinery can undertake selected applications of PRA we are not in a position to arrive at conclusions regarding country-level applications of PRA. National Statistical Organisations can plan for applications of PRA methods on scales larger than that provided by field evidence given above. This would happen only when the official machinery is convinced of major advantages emanating from use of PRA method such as quickness of data or depth of data as compared to those of the conventional questionnaire survey which they generally use.

In the context of large scale applications of PRA method one needs to look into the possibilities of purposive sampling in case it is not possible to repeat PRA exercises for each and every community/household. Such sampling can help in scaling of results in absence of complete coverage of households while steps can be taken to minimise the possibilities of sampling bias. Such sampling is implicit in the study by Haddad *et al.* (1993), NCAER (1993) and Adams *et al.* (1993) where PRA results have been generalised on that basis. The 'cost' and 'time' factors for application of PRA method on a large scale involving a large number of villages and their constituent households may pose to be a major consideration for most organisations. Hence, the scope of sampling for purposes of scaling up of PRA needs to be explored through field studies. More evidence is also required on the representativeness of the results of PRA through sampling procedures.

**Process and Flexibility**

As regards the process of data collection, the issue is how does it influence the output or the data collected. Some studies have emphasised the comparative processes involved in the two methods.

For instance, Haddad *et al.* (1993) while comparing PRA and conventional survey on the basis of fields results describes survey as mostly a question and answer session without a chance for discussion while PRA makes for open discussion, and answers get reasoning due to such discussion. In comparison, a conventional survey does not pay much attention to 'how' and 'why'.

In PRA method, the way is through the process of rapport building with local people which enables them to express themselves, set data in the context and make their own analysis to prove their point. Open-ended questions leave scope for greater probing and the flexibility inherent in PRA approach can adjust to multiple requirements unlike that of questionnaire survey. The process is such that it creates scope for new techniques to be invented for analysis. PRA method enables the communities to make their own analysis and the PRA process involves them in data generation.

**Does PRA have 'Elements' borrowed from Questionnaire Survey?**

On a close observation of the different studies reviewed above, one can find that many studies have combined 'elements' of conventional survey with PRA. As a result most of the PRA studies described in Chapter 2 have shown use of structured process, techniques and analysis. The elements of such structuring, however, vary within the broad limits of flexibility as provided by PRA. These elements have been traced out in some of the studies as indicated below:

**CASE 1**

ActionAid, Nepal(1992) combined some features of conventional survey with PRA. In line with conventional survey, the indicators for PRA survey were decided from the 'top' rather than by the local communities. The indicators were in three categories to be assessed for implementation, utilization and impact. As far as the process and techniques in the study are concerned one finds a large element of structuring of PRA guidelines similar to that in questionnaire surveys. The emphasis was on collecting relevant information as per the guidelines which made for considerable structuring from one sub-theme to another. For example, different social dimensions were to be shown in village maps followed by a list of development programmes and then indicators were to be identified for successful and unsuccessful groups and so on. Almost all the PRA techniques were structured for example, in case of village mapping detailed guidelines were provided on what the village map should contain and how to proceed (See Appendix 'A').

Hence the flexibility which one enjoys in application of PRA techniques and their sequencing was curtailed to a large extent for the sake of approaching uniformity in data collection especially for a 100 per cent coverage of households in Sindhupur Chowk. This also reduced the scope for innovation of the participants in terms of methods and output. At the same time the element of 'commonality' running through conventional questionnaire was maintained to some degree by structuring the techniques and providing detailed guidelines.

However, ActionAid Nepal's study was aimed at raising community awareness and understanding of utilisation of community services and hence was not extractive or limited to data collection only.

**CASE 2**

The study by Haddad *et al.* (1993) is one step forward to that of ActionAid, Nepal (1993) where alternative indicators for food and nutrition monitoring and evaluation system were not suggested from 'top' but were proposed to be identified by PRA to track movements in traditional indicators. The subtle elements of structuring were in terms of direction of probing and some 'typical' open questions to follow the visual technique (See Appendix 'A'). For this study, record forms were devised in the image of questionnaire schedules and proformas but they were there to provide basic guidelines for the PRA sessions for them to be flexible and open-ended. As far as the PRA techniques are concerned it was a specific set of techniques to be used by the investigators which had some semblance to a specific set of questionnaire to be filled during a questionnaire survey. Quantitative expression of indicators was also implied in the study. Hence, scoring was fixed in terms of number of seeds to be used so that quantitative weighting could take place.

Another point to reckon with is that in Haddad *et al.*'s study PRA method was essentially meant for data collection similar to a questionnaire survey and was extractive in that sense. Both in terms of process and application of techniques the study was not geared towards community participation. The study left little scope for people's priorities or actions so as to enhance their well being in terms of food security.

### CASE 3

Shah's (1993) paper showed the possibility of having questionnaires with participation and visual interaction. His paper showed that research can be initiated through an open-ended process in which people are given an opportunity to participate in designing of a questionnaire, developing criteria and indicators, discussing the issues to be explored and the data to be collected. The analysis can be through using a range of verbal and visual methods including questionnaires. Similarly Shah brought to fore the techniques of impact diagramming as another participatory method to indicate the impact of development activities. These include components like households, resources, livelihoods, environment, education, investment etc. These, with the help of group interactions are included in the checklist for individual interactions so as to enable local groups to be involved in discussing and prioritising the variables while individual interactions are initiated. It helps in asking a range of questions during individual interactions and reduces question fatigue. Additional aspects are included in the checklist for individual interaction.

Shah (1993) described the evolving of a visually interactive questionnaire where issues described by people during group discussions and other interactions are collated and presented to groups to develop a common understanding of the issues. At this stage, the outsiders are encouraged to add issues after explaining reason for such inclusion. For visual presentation, people develop symbols for different aspects of household profile and impact which are then used for information collection and analysis. Questionnaires on such a basis create scope for participants to exercise choice of responding through visual outputs with open ended interviews.

Shah's note is centered on developing questionnaire with continuous re-iterations so as to make the questionnaire more realistic, participatory, visually interactive and self-corrected. Hence, Shah's study, discusses a mode of questionnaire totally different from the structured questionnaire of the conventional survey.

**CASE 4**

The study by Adams *et al.* (1993) starts with an open-ended process and uses participatory techniques extensively both with groups and individuals to arrive at its results. The importance of observation and probing are also emphasised as a part of informal inquiry. The study is on the look out for a measure of well being and arrives at a composite measure of household well being based on a number of indicators as emerging from the study. The problem with composite indicators is that by clubbing of indicators they tend to get aggregated and the scope for diversity gets reduced. For composite indicators, the emphasis is on aggregation by which we tend to lose information by aggregating and averaging.

Again, the study has revealed its preference towards quantification in the shadow of conventional inquiry. When using matrix ranking in health service utilisation the kind of scoring is predetermined by the study where scoring is done out of a fixed number of 20 seeds.

In this section, we find that many PRA studies have selected different features of conventional survey to be combined with PRA method for different results. The studies have borrowed such features and have built on them to make their study not only participatory and meaningful but also precise in design and manageability. I have indicated below such traces of characteristics of conventional survey in PRA method as evident from the field studies.

**Images of Conventional Surveys to be Found in PRA Studies**

* Structured guidelines
* Specific forms to be filled and questions to be answered
* Indicators suggested from 'top' to be tested through PRA
* Stress on quantitative data

* Fixed set of techniques to be used
* No scope for sequencing of methods by participants
* Data collection extractive and used by outsiders to local communities

In contrast to the above, we also find the 'essence' of PRA method present in these studies which make them distinct from conventional surveys and bring them under the umbrella of PRA studies. Some of these are as follows:

* Use of checklists
* Open-ended questions
* Group interviews and interactions
* Use of a range of participatory techniques
* Visual techniques followed by verbal interactions
* both qualitative and quantitative data
* absence of rigorous sampling
* emphasis on disaggregation of data
* enabling people to participate
* Learning being continuous and iterative
* Raising of community awareness and understanding through participation.

The field-based studies under consideration have made adjustments in terms of flexibility, created scope for innovativeness, people's analysis and linked-up process and participatory design in order to gain in terms of data management, specific responses and descriptive statistics.

**Methods, Depth (Dimensions)**

The issue is what kind of data is important for any data collection exercise. Much depends on whether we want descriptive or analytical statistics or both. The method involved in any kind of data collection generally has an influence on the kind of output, its range and its depth. With closed and fixed set of questions in the conventional inquiry we look for precise and fixed answers and mostly for quantification in terms of numbers. In this way, a good deal of information on linkage and process are lost, qualitative answers tend to get overlooked and outliers tend to get marginalised.

The study by Rajaratnam *et al.* (1993) on PRA technique of wealth ranking shows gender differences which otherwise would have remained hidden. Men, appeared not so interested and while doing the wealth ranking were concerned more with levels of agricultural production, nature of land, possession of livestock, employment and sources of income. The women, on the other hand, were relatively more open and had enough information on intricate details on each household which had a bearing on wealth. Their knowledge showed depth. They went into details of categories of poor from one layer to the other.

In the studies reviewed earlier, different PRA techniques were used extensively to collect both qualitative and quantitative data. In this connection, Shah (1993) points out that questionnaire surveys, are basically capable of providing limited information which are neither analytical nor visually interactive. While PRA techniques provide different dimensions of information. For example, mapping helps in locating households, selection of sample and establishing rapport whereas seasonality helps to project seasonal behaviour of different variables. PRA techniques enjoy the flexibility of generating a variety of information on different aspects of any issue for which a questionnaire survey is of limited use by its very approach of having structured questions and absence of visual interaction.

*Output*

A comparison of output in the two methods under consideration raises issues like the nature and form of output, its utility, its accuracy and reliability. On the nature and form of output, some field studies have compared the output generated by the two methods and have made different observations. Here are a few of them.

Fry and McCabe (1986) commented on the over-simplification of information by macro surveys. They, in their paper on movements of pastoral Turkana of Kenya, based on both micro and macro study, concluded that "macro surveys tend to produce information resembling ideal behaviour by collapsing incomplete data sets into generalized patterns of action whereas micro studies tend to result in detailed accounts based on the actual behaviour of a limited number of individuals." Development projects in arid and semi-arid regions are usually based on the premise that pastoralists behave as a group. The macro approach to data collection reinforce this concept by generalizing individual behaviour patterns. Moves involving only small groups are suggested as anomalous and contradictory behaviour. Frequently macro analysis assume that data of this type represent errors based on misinformation which are then removed from the results. But these apparently irregular behaviour patterns may, in fact, be of key importance to a full understanding of pastoral movements. Fry and McCabe hold that over-simplification of macro surveys can be misleading and can give rise to basic conceptualisation of development schemes alien to the traditional pastoralist system.

Colfer *et al.* (1987) described their experience with two complementary approaches in involving Indonesian farmers in soil management research, under Tropsoils (is the popular name for USAID's Collaborative Research Support Programme on Soil Management also called the Soil's CRSP) of which the first one is a collaborative mode in which farmers and scientists try to design and implement experiments on farmer's fields and the second one is a focused study using social science methods to understand social science methods. The study concluded that if collaborative research with farmers is possible it seems to provide a more direct, personal experience type involvement for scientists --- providing direct feedback on the topic that is most important to them (their experiments).

The study by Adams *et al.* (1993) states that conventional quantitative methods are appropriate to undertake tasks of measuring impact of socio-economic development on health and well being. However, in order to investigate dynamic pathways of change, an imaginative and transdisciplinary approach to research design is required which express questions and hypotheses with an innovative blend of qualitative and quantitative methods.

### *Utility*

As far as utility of methods is concerned, Shah (1993), while commenting on the output produced by local community through PRA, writes that the community owns the output it produces and it is empowering for the community to use such data for making their plans of action.

Much depends on the expected utility of the data generated. If some policy needs to be designed based on descriptive statistics then conventional survey can be conducted for such purpose whereas for policy making based on linkages and processes incorporating local people's criteria and views it appears that use of PRA method is indispensable.

*Accuracy and Evaluation*

There are two basic questions with regard to evaluation of data and accuracy of output. One is the issue as to whether PRA data can be evaluated and cross-checked, two, is whether PRA results are more accurate than conventional surveys and three, is the degree of accuracy possible with PRA data.

**Criteria for Evaluation**

With regard to the first question it may be said that different criteria of evaluation can be applied to PRA data and there are a variety of checks and balances for cross-checking of data collected. The studies from the field have actually demonstrated a variety of methods used for such cross-checking some of which are described below.

**CASE 1**

Two different sources were used by Rajaratnam *et al.* (1993) for obtaining all kinds of information regarding the economic levels of households after which the investigators verified those houses whose classification differed as per the sources. The results were verified through observation of people in the household, the household assets, the structure of the house, discussion with people in the house, health volunteer, rural community organiser and influential leaders.

**CASE 2**

Haddad *et al.* (1993) continuously verified the results by different approaches which were five in number -- the nutrition survey, economic survey, PRA method, ethnography and serum analysis.

For overcoming the seasonal bias of the survey it was conducted in rounds which represented both peak and lean periods of food production and labour demand and also a round of 'medium production and high morbidity'. For offsetting gender bias, the survey performed gender-related contrasts.

PRA method was used to check survey results and record forms were devised for PRA exercises. Cross-checking was in-built into the PRA guidelines at each stage via groups, investigators, methods, seasons, and places. There was scope for cross-checking of PRA data by participants which also included gender-checking.

**CASE 3**

Adams *et al.* (1993) designed the study so as to include triangulation of data by methods, sources, 'peer debriefing' sessions in the evening and participant checking to summarise and evaluate discussions.

## Is PRA Method More Accurate than Survey?

This is a complex question to answer because the relevant point is whose accuracy are we interested in. If we are looking at professional's accuracy in terms of preciseness to certain no. of decimal places then PRA results need not be accurate in that sense. On the other hand, if we are looking at ground level realities in terms of local people's estimates, measurements and comparisons then PRA results are trustworthy since they are generated by people to whom the data is related. Their accuracy is higher than that of professional estimates since it is first hand data generated by the local people with whom PRA is done. Here are some evidence from case studies.

**CASE 1**

Rajaratnam *et al.* (1993) pointed out that the indicators used in survey failed to reflect the real economic status. RUHSA's formal survey was extensively planned so as to ensure accuracy amongst other objectives. For such data collected there was emphasis on review meetings, editing, sample verification and supervision. The enumerators were educated and had 6 to 8 years experience in data collection besides experience in editing and coding of data.

The actual information on economic conditions varied from household to household and it was not easy to structure it uniformly in a schedule so as to include all possible information. In the event of inclusion of all possible information in a schedule, people would have been reluctant to supply the necessary information. Response rate, in such cases, was expected to be low and its accuracy doubtful and the process of analysis cumbersome.

In case of wealth ranking the information was obtained from knowledgeable informants of the same community on whom the principal investigators were dependent. Wealth ranking process brought out the true economic level through knowledge of the key informants. After different ways of validation, Rajaratnam *et al.*'s study (1993) concluded that knowledge of informants was a valid reflection of community's classification based on their having more accurate information.

**CASE 2**

In Adams *et al.*'s (1993) study there was relative consistency of male and female mapping. While comparing gender maps in Paboi, the number of households matched with the exception of one widowed household recognised only by women. Whereas, in case of Mohonpur, the same households were identified by men and women in 90 per cent of the cases. However, male participants showed a widowed household overlooked by women whereas female participants recognised three widowed households overlooked by men. In case of the number of married adults the gender maps coincided in 88 to 92 per cent of the cases.

**CASE 3**

NCAER (1993) pointed out that at village level, comparison of RRA/PRA based data on household numbers and population parameters with the 1991 census figures was found to show under ±10 per cent variation as against much larger variation in the village schedule–based data in the sample survey approach. Similarly RRA/PRA data aggregated at village level compared well with household based overall regional patterns. All these point to the reliability of RRA/PRA data.

NCAER (1993) also adds that, in situations, requiring information on a few variables like physical assets such as land, animals or for stratification/cross-classification of households PRA techniques like mapping and ranking exercises are reliable tools for data collection at village level. Otherwise, for many variables at the regional level, conventional sample surveys give better results.

In people's participation at the local level, it is important to consider people's perceptions as much as professional's perceptions since it is people who are the stakeholders in the development process. In case of discrepancies arising from the two sets of perceptions they can be resolved through cross checking or mutual process of conflict resolution. The following section describes some experiences on discrepancies of PRA and conventional survey data. It shows how, on many occasions PRA can help in clarifying conventional survey data.

**Discrepancy in Data: PRA–Type Inquiry and Conventional Survey**

**CASE 1**

Socio-economic and ecological information on a social forestry project through a RRA approach was compared to the results of a formal questionnaire survey conducted by a social forestry project in Sierra Leone, West Africa (Inglis: 1991). The biases of questionnaire survey, like local knowledge bias, seasonal bias, bias of resident people were offset to a large extent by RRA. The two results of questionnaire survey and RRA showed wide discrepancy for a major fuelwood using community called Tombo. The most preferred species was also different. There were many other discrepancies in the results relating to the preferences, the preferred species and the trading system. The study concluded that, in general, RRA was more efficient than the standard formal questionnaire.

**CASE 2**

According to NCAER (1993) conventional survey controls the 'variance' and imparts representative character to the findings wheras PRA controls non-sampling errors arising from interviewer/respondent biases. Information with contextual linkages enhances reliability and also provides insights while reporting on findings. There is a 'trade off' between the two approaches in statistical precision and quality of information.

After a discussion of field aspects involved in PRA as an alternative method to questionnaire survey I find that we require greater evidence from field aspects related to costs, in terms of national and regional level applications and management information systems on PRA. However, on the basis of the above discussion I can safely state the following for PRA as a method :

* PRA yields quicker output.
* PRA can be applied to large scale of inquiry and the scale of application has not yet been described as a limiting factor except for the element of cost, if any, on which we need more evidence from the field.
* Process of PRA is more flexible and can adjust to multiple requirements.
* Analytical ability of PRA techniques is greater and makes for

in-depth information
* In PRA, community analyses its own output.
* Cross-checking of data is possible in different ways in PRA output.
* Accuracy can be ensured for PRA data with the help of different ways.

In the event of similar costs for PRA and questionnaire survey, the choice is based on the strengths of PRA as a method of data collection. In the alternative scenario of relative costs of PRA being higher there is a 'trade off' between costs and benefits of PRA and depends on how big and significant the 'trade off' is to the people/institution concerned.

**Ownership and Empowerment**

Coming to ownership, PRA data are owned by local community and used by the community for its own betterment. It is the local community which participates in creating the data and hence naturally owns the data which it has created. As Shah (1993) points out the participatory techniques enable local functionaries to be facilitators and develop analytical abilities for future work. Such output enables local institutions to create locally based information systems and helps in their interface with outside agencies.

There is a process of empowerment involved for local community in creation of the data base and in a natural sequence, PRA would lead to community-based decision making and action. This, however, need not be followed in the course of using PRA method for data collection where people's participation is a one time exercise for obtaining such data. Hence, mere use of PRA method in data collection does not reach the climax of empowerment in terms of people's actions. It does empower local people to a limited extent in generating and creating their own data profiles which are then used by investigators and outside professionals for their own purposes.

**Learning**

Use of PRA method enhances the learning process and enriches the experience involved. The learning is due to the local community members' natural unfolding of their views, priorities and preferences. Such unfolding brings to the fore community experience which otherwise remain hidden. Structured questions can help in partial projection of such experience and gain as well as lose information in the process. This loss of information is hedged against in PRA by letting community members have a natural flow to describe experiences undergone by them, their views and other related aspects. The learning process is wholesome and iterative.

**Summary**

In this chapter, PRA-type inquiry is posed as an alternative to questionnaire survey. With a spectrum of experience in PRA method, different aspects of PRA have been examined in order to draw interim conclusions on comparative issues like cost, time, training, scale of inquiry, process, flexibility, depth, utility, trustworthiness, empowerment and learning. For some issues like cost and scaling up at the country level, we require further evidence so as to draw general conclusions. Whereas, for other issues like time, process, flexibility, depth, utility, learning, trustworthiness and empowerment we have experiences which weigh considerably in favour of PRA-type inquiry.

# 5

# SUMMARY AND CONCLUSIONS

In this chapter, I summarise the results obtained in the earlier chapters and the lessons learnt in the area of methodological issues. Inter-comparison of major field studies as discussed in Chapters 2, 3 and 4 are summarised in this chapter in order to draw comparative evidence in different aspects of field inquiry. The different studies reviewed in Chapter 2 had different objectives to pursue, such as identifying indicators, assessing community utilisation of assets and services, making a comparative study of questionnaire survey and PRA-type inquiry and other objectives. However, the thread which is common to such studies is that of conducting a participatory type of inquiry. The following sections compare such studies with regard to their objectives, size, location, duration, techniques and other aspects.

## Inter-Comparison of Field Studies

**Table 5.1**

**Case Studies : Major Objectives**

Haddad *et al.* (1993)

* to identify alternative indicators for use in food and nutrition monitoring and evaluation systems

ActionAid, Nepal (1992)

* to assess community utilisation of assets and services
* to increase community understanding of its own development for better planning and implementation

Rajaratnam *et al.* (1993)

* to identify community indicators for economic status and to validate professional's classification with community classification in wealth ranking of households

Adams *et al.* (1993)

* to assess effectiveness of participatory techniques in collecting information and to identify indigenous indicators of health, wealth and women's status

contd.....

Inglis (1991)

* to collect socio-economic and socio-ecological information by RRA for direct comparison with questionnaire survey
* to provide accurate information regarding fuelwood marketing structure and species preference validation in selected locations

Ṣhah (1993)

* to evolve and use visually interactive and participatory methods through an open-ended process so as to enhance communication between the researcher and the respondent

ActionAid, Pakistan (1993/94)

* to discern and identify causes of poverty and groups of very poor
* to understand poverty as a series of interlinked social, economic, environmental and political conditions

Zafer (1993)

* to understand the concept of knowledge sharing within the community and groups regarding the water sector, particularly the functioning of Water Committees to understand their impact on community level decision making

NCAER (1992/1993)

* to examine efficacy of complementing or substituting sample surveys with PRAs based on comparisons of results relating to reliability level of data sets, cost/time trade offs, quality of field workers, training components etc.

Buchanan-Smith *et al.* (1993)

* to understand how people perceive and prioritise their food security problems.

**Table 5.2**

**Case Studies : Size, Location and Duration of PRA-Type Inquiry**

Haddad *et al.* (1993)

* conducted in 4 Indian villages of Andhra Pradesh and Maharashtra, India

ActionAid, Nepal (1992)

* conducted in 9 Gaon Bikas Samiti in Rural Development Area of Sindhupal

Chowk, Nepal consisting of 6544 households

* duration of one week (including 3 days for training and one day for discussion of findings)

Rajaratnam *et al.* (1993)

* conducted in Maliapattu panchayat at Tamil Nadu, India; covering 412 households in Maliapattu Panchayat of Tamil Nadu, India

Adams *et al.* (1993)

* conducted in Matlab Thana, Bangladesh in two villages, Paboi and Mohonpur at Jamalpur for 5 days followed by 2 days of analysis and writing up

Inglis (1991)

* conducted in one village (Moyeimi), 3 small towns (Fogbo, Newton and Songo) and one large town (Tombo) for a period of three weeks

Shah (1993)

* undertaken in Bharuch District (Gujarat), India

ActionAid, Pakistan (1993/94)

* conducted in 11 villages with a population of approximately 38,000 in Kalinger Union Council in North Pakistan

contd.....

Zafer (1993)

* conducted in 69 communities of Northern Punjab and Azad Jammu & Kashmir

NCAER (1993)

* 10 villages in Maharashtra for 30 days

Buchanan-Smith *et al.* (1993)

* 55 villages and a number of towns

---

**Table 5.3**

**Case Studies : PRA Techniques Used**

---

Haddad *et al.* (1993)

* mapping, food charts, women's activity charts and seasonality charts

ActionAid, Nepal (1992)

* village mapping, semi-structured interviews, seasonal analysis, time trend and preference ranking

Rajaratnam *et al.* (1993)

* wealth ranking

Adams *et al.* (1993)

* social and demographic mapping, health and wealth pile-sort ranking health service utilisation matrix ranking, time line and focus group discussions, key informant interviews and life histories of women

Inglis (1991)

* interviews, mapping, preference pair ranking, indicator identification, fuelwood measurement and direct observation

Shah (1993)

* visually interactive questionnaire and impact diagramming

ActionAid, Pakistan (1993/94)

* wealth ranking

Zafar (1993)

* household questionnaires, three dimensional model set, decision making process with visuals and rating matrix with a three scale grid

NCAER (1992/93)

* mapping, transect walks, historical transect, timeliness, group discussions and semi-structured interviews

Buchanan-Smith *et al.* (1993)

* semi-structured interviews, ranking and prioritisation

---

**Table 5.4**

**Case Studies : Elements of Conventional Inquiry**

---

Haddad *et al.* (1993)

* direction of probing is structured; set of 'open' questions are structured to follow the visuals
* record forms devised to provide basic guidelines -- a specific set of methods used, scoring is quantitative based on a fixed number of seeds

ActionAid, Nepal (1992)

* indicators decided from 'top';
* structuring of guidelines for collection of relevant information;
* structuring of guidelines from one sub-theme to another;
* structuring of PRA techniques and their dimensions

Rajaratnam *et al.* (1993)

* household listing from conventional survey used for classifying households by PRA wealth ranking

Adams *et al.* (1993)

* to arrive at a composite measure of household well being based on a number of indicators emerging from the study;
* there is also quantified scoring in terms of fixed number of seeds

Inglis (1991)

* for comparing RRA with conventional survey for adopting an appropriate strategy for marketing of fuelwood
* visual maps were improvised and amended by the investigators
* investigators also limited the scope of pairwise ranking

Shah (1993)

* query in form of a questionnaire

Zafar (1993)

* household questionnaire was a part of participatory techniques
* techniques and their use were fixed by investigators

ActionAid, Pakistan (1993/94)

* sampling of key informants for wealth ranking

NCAER (1992/93)

* non-probabilistic sampling for districts, stratified random sampling for villages

Buchanan-Smith *et al.* (1993)

* villages not decided by people but by purposive sampling
* visual and digrammatic techniques almost absent
* results not presented to local people

---

**Table 5.5**

**Case Studies : Problems Faced and Lessons Learnt**

ActionAid, Nepal (1992)

* indicators decided from 'top' for the sake of having universal indicators, inadequate training, guidelines used as questionnaires, shortage of time, open-endedness of questions leading to varied levels/kinds of information
* Lessons learnt that analysis and management of data need to be emphasised, process of analysis should be left to survey team who are nearer to the field

Rajaratnam *et al.* (1993)

* Informant's bias in classifying their and their relation's households
* Lessons learnt that informants for wealth ranking are those residing in the community for 15 to 20 years and having detailed knowledge; in PRA.
* The programme implementators directly in the field have better understanding of the community

Adams *et al.* (1993)

* Lessons are that location of group work in quiet, shady places is critical for success of PRA; active effort required to limit participation to gender groups;
* wealth ranking may be sensitive and require long explanations, social mapping useful for locating households, for sample selection and building rapport, observational studies within households are also required

Inglis (1991)

* repetition of techniques frequently became tedious
* results of conventional questionnaire survey and RRA method regarding preferred species and ranking of location were at variance with each other
* in case of erroneous RRA results it was possible to recheck them by talking to different groups of people whereas in case of conventional survey it was not easy to correct omissions and inaccuracies through statistical manipulations

NCAER (1992/93)

* RRA/PRA need not be suitable for application at national/state/regional level due to its present character of village level application
* The problem of wider applicability can be overcome by integrating RRA/PRA with conventional survey
* RRA/PRA can be effectively employed for monitoring and evaluation of different variables and their linkages
* Techniques of RRA/PRA to be effective need a lot of experience
* For larger level applications, time and cost factors can limit the use of RRA/PRA

Buchanan-Smith *et al.* (1993)

* enumerator bias difficult to overcome
* with limited time and resources RRA survey can be large in size
* RRA survey conducted in a drought year have impact on the results
* huge amount of qualitative information can be unwieldy and difficult to handle

**Table 5.6**

**Case Studies : Evaluation of Data**

Haddad *et al.* (1993)

* cross-checking was in-built into guidelines at each point whether via groups, investigators, techniques, seasons, places, note taking or while moving from one 'visual' to another 'visual' of the same kind. The project has included cross-checking of PRA data by participants as well as checking by gender.

ActionAid, Nepal (1992)

* cross-checking of data was done through identification of gaps by re-checking/processing of data and bringing them back to the village and filling them up

Rajaratnam *et al.* (1993)

* validation of classification of households by local groups was undertaken by cross checking it with different groups of informants

Adams *et al.* (1993)

* the study design incorporated triangulation in the form of different sources of information, different techniques were used including 'peer debriefing' sessions of the investigators
* the study also used participant checking to summarise and evaluate discussions

Inglis (1991)

* the research bias of conventional survey such as main road bias, local knowledge bias and seasonal bias were taken care of by the RRA team

Shah (1993)

* essentially based on participant cross-checking

ActionAid, Pakistan (1993/94)

* cross-checking by means of different informants

Zafer (1993)

* cross-checking of data through different sources such as male groups, female groups and households

NCAER (1992/93)

* validation of data by different techniques, groups and places and by results of conventional survey

Buchanan-Smith *et al.* (1993)

* Interviews with groups followed by cross-checking with households especially females
* triangulation on the basis of three different years of rainfall

The above tables provide summary results of an inter-comparison of field studies with regard to various aspects of such studies. From the discussion of studies, as indicated in Chapters 2, 3 and 4, one can observe many combinations of 'elements' of conventional survey with 'elements' of a PRA-type inquiry and permutations of a PRA-type inquiry itself. The issue is whether it is possible to draw some more lessons and conclusions with regard to the options available regarding field inquiry based on the field studies reviewed. On the basis of learning from such field studies, I suggest a broad outline for a participatory-type field inquiry with different combinations and options possible.

## Checklist for a Participatory Field Inquiry

The checklist for a participatory-type field inquiry would go broadly by the following steps wherein, each step envisages a series of alternatives in the form of a spectrum revolving around people's participation. Such a spectrum ranges on the degree of participation from a lower end of people's participation to a higher end of such participation. The sequencing of steps, however, would vary from one study to another in the direction of identifying the following:

* a theme
* its significance
* its nature and scope
* its purpose
* kinds of queries and probing
* form/forms of output
* for whom is the output ?
* designing a plan for inquiry
* time required
* assessing training needs
* methods/techniques used
* process in field inquiry
* cross-checking of data & process
* techniques of cross-checking
* utility of output
* management/organization of data

*Theme*

To begin with any inquiry process it is important that the theme is stated and clarified whether by researchers, local community or both.

* Description of the issue/problem/theme of the field inquiry; in a participatory mode, such description if provided by local people would be more participatory, realistic and of direct relevance to the project.

*Significance*

Once a theme is stated, its significance also needs to be described whether by researchers or the local community involved. Much depends on whether the theme is significant at the national level or is locally significant.

* Description of the significance of the issue/problem/theme; such significance if described by local people would reflect their perceptions and views and initiate local participation from the very start. Or alternatively, to initiate a participatory-type of inquiry, the local people would need to be motivated on a theme which is not of much relevance to them.

*Nature and Scope of Inquiry*

* The issue and its significance would determine the nature of inquiry whether exploratory, topical, evaluative or of other kind. In PRA, the nature of inquiry can also be suggested by the local people and led and conducted by them if the purpose of the field inquiry is properly clarified to them.
* For kind of output required—is it statistical representation with high degree of accuracy?/is it levels or process of change or both?/ what is the unit of analysis-individuals, households, communities? and what kind of community involvement is expected in data collection and analysis.

*Purpose*

* On the basis of any issue and its significance as suggested by researchers/local people, the purpose of inquiry can be described by the research organization/local people or jointly by both and its objective(s) formulated. If the objectives of the organization for the project are already existing they can be revised in the light of local people's wisdom to the extent possible.

*Kind of Queries and Probing*

* Description of the questions to be asked, the output required and the user-groups can be determined by researchers/local people or jointly in collaboration with the organization/researchers involved.

*Form of Output*

* The different stages of field inquiry involved can evoke contributions of local groups and of outside organization. The kind of output may or may not be pre-determined by researchers/local community in terms

of descriptive statistics/analytical data. It can be quantitative/qualitative or a combination of both depending on the needs of the organization and the preferences and capabilities of the local people.

*For Whom is the Output?*

* Description of the form in which the output/data is to be organised and accessed or the management information system required by the local people/local institutions/researchers or by others. For this the relevant questions are, is the output to be taken away from the local community and processed further or is it to be retained at the local level for initiating further action or is it a combination of both ?

*Time/Manpower/Funds Required*

* Description of the time required/available, manpower required/ available and funds required/available for the inquiry and the contributions which local community and outside researchers can make, if necessary.

*Designing a Plan for Inquiry*

* Definition of the area of coverage/complete enumeration/sampling frame --the size of the area and the sampling procedure to be followed whether probabilistic sampling or non-probabilistic sampling. In PRA–type inquiry, non-probabilistic sampling for identifying sampling units like regions, districts, blocks, villages and focus groups may be more effective to take care of the differences existing between the sampling units.

Once districts and blocks have been selected one can apply a set of criteria for selection of villages (especially when differences between villages are considerable) in terms of size, level of development, social and ethnic groups, degree of problem under consideration, distance from main road and road conditions and other criteria. Purposive sampling can help in offsetting road-side bias, seasonal bias, people's bias, project bias and others. For instance, for offsetting seasonal bias the study can be conducted in more than one season. There can also be sampling of participants/respondents/ key informants for offsetting people's bias. In this context, one can look at the background of the area, the secondary data and other materials and sources of indigenous knowledge, history and culture.

For studies involving large areas, the researchers can design sampling to cover different aspects required and let the local community decide on a design once it comes to conducting an inquiry at a local level. Or, the researchers can revise their design on learning from local community members. For this purpose, apart from the secondary data, initial interviewing of selected key informants and other local people may be helpful to start with. This would help to know more about the villages to be considered. In case of a questionnaire survey, questionnaires can be designed and re-designed in this manner and tested for field level applications.

Next, is to decide on the mode of coverage, whether by sampling or complete enumeration. If one decides on sampling the units, then one needs to decide on each stage of sampling to pass from larger units to smaller units for better interaction. If a topic is focussed then sampling of focus groups and informants can also help in generation of better information and saving of time.

*Assessing Training Needs*

* Assessment of training needs required for principal and co-facilitators whether outsiders or local people or a combination of both, and the duration and the kind of training possible with given resources. For large scale of inquiry one needs to look into multiplying training inputs in a short period of time. This may be possible with training of principal facilitators who, in turn, train the co-facilitators. Inclusion of local people in the inquiry team can help in multiplying the impact of training and in periodic upgradation of data at the local level.

*Investigators/Teams*

One can go single or form teams for going into villages, with necessary accessories like notebooks, paper, pens, supportive materials for 'visual' output etc. The teams can have a combination of the following:

* questionnaire to be filled up
* checklists
* record forms to be filled up which can be a combination of questions and guidelines/checklists
* blank note books and other supporting materials
* other items which are thought to be necessary.

The teams can be a combination of outside researchers of different disciplines, of men and women, or a combination of outside researchers and local people or exclusively consisting of local people themselves.

*Methods/Techniques Used in Field Inquiry*

There are many possibilities in running either a PRA-type inquiry or a questionnaire survey or a combination of the two. Some of these are as follows:

* canvassing of a questionnaire
* testing a questionnaire and re-designing it with PRA techniques and canvassing it
* using both household questionnaire and PRA techniques for inquiry
* using selected PRA techniques for complementing survey data
* using list of households surveyed as basis for applying PRA techniques like wealth ranking, social mapping and others
* using one or more of PRA techniques
* sequencing of PRA techniques by sequentially passing from one technique to another
* evolving a questionnaire by PRA techniques which is visually interactive

*Process in Field Inquiry*

The process in a field inquiry would differ from situation to situation. The process involves rapport building in case of a PRA-type inquiry. The rapport building can be in various ways in order to establish effective community dialogue some of which are as follows. Probing is better in an open and relaxed manner in a natural setting and would include meeting local individuals and groups.

The process of probing, using PRA techniques and sequencing them are integral parts of a PRA-type inquiry. The process of initiating people's action and sustaining them is equally important for PRA. PRA revolves around people's initiative, efforts and actions keeping in view the objectives considered:

* meeting individual respondent for filling questionnaire
* meeting individual participant for PRA sessions e.g., in case studies

* meeting both groups and individuals in PRA sessions
* meeting the groups gender-wise or meeting other focus groups.

*Cross-Checking of Data and its Process*

Cross-checking of data and its process can happen as an on-going activity or towards the end of the study. Cross-checking is required to establish the trustworthiness of any study, to fill gaps and to improve the quality of the study. The local people can themselves do the cross-checking. In this context, there can be three kinds of cross-checking whether done by investigators/researchers or local people or a combination of both:

* Continuous cross-checking
* Cross-checking and filling gaps at the end
* Cross-checking at selected stages.

*Techniques of Cross-Checking*

The techniques of cross-checking data can also be of different kinds, such as,

* Triangulation of techniques where different techniques, sources, time and places are used
* participant checking
* Checking with conventional survey data
* Checking with other sources, earlier findings
* Peer group checking.

*Utility of Output*

The output generated through a PRA-type inquiry can be used in diverse ways. An ideal way would be to empower and enable the community to use it for its own betterment. Some of the ways of using the data collected are as follows:

* To enable local people to own it and use in their own plans and projects
* To use it for local projects managed from outside
* To create data base
* To use it for further research
* To test results of conventional surveys
* To test PRA findings.

*Management/Organisation of Data*

Data generated can be varied and large in a PRA-type field inquiry. It can relate to several dimensions of human and natural resources, technology, institutions and others and organising such data at an individual, household, community, village and/or regional level is a complicated task given the nature of data, both qualitative and quantitative with little or no structuring of schedules to suggest uniform patterns of data collection. Planning for management of data is a crucial learning point from field studies. If the management of data is not planned properly then large amounts of data can be lost/wasted. To take care of problems in data management one can make an initial design for management of data to start with. The charts and maps made by local community members can be preserved with care at the local level for future use and can be updated at that level from time to time. The processing can be manual or computer-based depending on facilities available with the organization in charge of data collection.

## Concluding Remarks

There are various considerations for conducting either a questionnaire survey or a PRA-type inquiry or both together and arrive at ways to approach a problem at hand for which data collection becomes an essential requirement to start with. It is important to remember that data collection whether through questionnaire survey or PRA method involves basic issues in cost, time, scale, utility, depth and other aspects. In addition, whatever be the size of data collection it is important to approach it in such a manner so as to achieve a reasonable level of trustworthiness.

With regard to PRA as an independent method of inquiry, recent field experiences, as described in Chapters 2, 3 and 4, show that it is possible to use PRA-type inquiry to conduct large scale data collection and get quicker results with deeper analysis. However, further investigation is needed for dimensions of cost, sampling and handling of diverse data sets in addition to the ones which we already have.

In this context, some other issues thrown up for discussion are ways to approach big villages and larger populations and scale up applications of PRA-type inquiry. The issue for the politician and macro planner is how to arrive at population characteristics at a regional level/country level for mesho and macro level decision making. This also needs further field investigations and offers another area which requires researching. Still another interesting aspect of the methodologies for data collection is that of sharing and communication between innovators, researchers and practitioners of the fruits of inter-disciplinary research which can be disseminated through networking and improved upon.

Each opportunity for data collection opens up a range of potential for further innovations in the field. We saw earlier in Chapter 3, that on many occasions use of participatory inquiry and questionnaire survey together actually combine individual features for complementing each other and re-inforcing the data set created in the process. Field experience indicate that questionnaire surveys can be combined with PRA-type inquiry for better results (gaining in terms of efficient design, quality of data, less time, depth and trustworthiness). Whereas, PRA–type inquiry can have elements borrowed from conventional inquiry which impact on its process and output, they also help in data from becoming unwieldy and add to convenience in management and handling of data.

For any type of field inquiry, it is best to approach it with an open mind and explore a few questions in order to know more as to why an inquiry is being conducted, what are its objectives, what is the output required, in what form, for whom (the users) and when. All these questions can then be weighed for considerations such as time, cost, quality, quantity trustworthiness of data and the like. As such there are no simple answers existing to guide field level inquiry since the requirements, objectives, constraints, options and conditions operating for a field inquiry differ from situation to situation and in each case it is best to make a pragmatic assessment of the situation at hand and deliver meaningful results whether through exclusive application or combination of the methods at hand.

*APPENDIX A*

# A-1

## EXTRACTS FROM UTILIZATION SURVEY, 1991
## ACTIONAID, NEPAL (AAN)

### A GUIDELINE
### RURAL DEVELOPMENT AREA, SINDHUPALCHOWK

**"This note briefly explains about the purpose and methods of the utilization survey that we are undertaking this year.**

**Objectives**

1. To assess how far the ideas and assets which the community has developed with AAN are being utilized, and what impact this is having on the conditions of community, as perceived by community.
2. To increase the community's understanding of and sense of responsibility for its own development, and through this to make the planning and implementation processes more effective.
3. To increase the understanding of the poorest people's problems and needs by both AAN staff and other members of the community, to establish the idea of focusing on the poorest in the CDC.
4. To know how much AAN programmes are benefiting and involving the poorest members of the community in relation to other members, and to understand why AAN programmes are not reaching the poorest.

**Day First**

1. Draw village map.

— Indicate path, tap stand, Chautari, school, day care centre, health centre etc.

— Show each house.

— Write the names of household heads on the map.

— Note the number of family members in each household (give separate symbols for recording female, male, children below 15 and 5 years.)

(One map may consist of about 100 houses. Maps of the wards having more or less houses than 100, can be adjusted accordingly)

2. Make a list of development programmes implemented in the village. Distinguish the activities implemented by ActionAid.

— List of the development programmes should be made according to villagers' perception and memory.

— List them according to villagers' priority order.

— Only the open questions should be asked.

— Make separate list of programmes not mentioned by the villagers, if the survey team knows about it.

**Second Day**

*Community Motivation and Training*

1. Explain the village map. Find out the following about the users group.
2. Indicate the various groups existing in the village map.
3. Make a circle mark to identify the households in each group.
4. Identify the indicators of successful and unsuccessful groups for group effectiveness and participation. (For example questions should begin with how, and what)
5. Rank the groups on the basis of relative effectiveness. Ranking may be recorded on the map by giving symbols.
6. The indicators of group effectiveness should be noted, by the teachers on separate sheet of paper.

*Education Programme*

1. Explain the village map. Indicate the following on the map:
   — Schools (with number of class rooms)
   — Number of the school going children in each household.
   — Number of students above five class in each household.
   — Number of the CLC graduates who are still literate.
   — Number of the ALC graduates who are still literate.
   — Mark the place where HRCs are running.
2. Prepare a time trend for following:
   — Standard of the student's education.
   — School attendance

— Use of educational extracurricular materials.

*Community Technical Service*

1. Explain the village map.
2. Recheck and confirm the indication of tapstand spots.
3. Make a circle for the households getting drinking water facilities from each tap.
4. Indicate the taps with no water.
5. Indicate the tapstands requiring maintenance.
6. Show the bridges on resource village map.
7. Show the multipurpose power unit (MPPU) on the resource map.
8. Indicate the trails rennovated.

**Third Day**

*Health Programme*

1. Explain the village map.
2. Indicate the household visiting health post, mobile clinic, and other various health camps.
3. Indicate the places of health posts, mobile clinic, and various health camps.
4. Indicate the households using pit latrines for more than a year.
5. Indicate the households using family planning methods regularly. Note the birth spacing between the last two children.
6. Indicate the households using the smokeless chulos.
7. Record the number of children, below one year, in each household.
8. Record the number below 5-year children who are already immunized.
9. Record the number below 1-year children, who are getting immunization.
10. Record the number of children attending DCC regularly.
11. Indicate the households providing support to DCC regularly (i.e. *Khaja*).
12. Record the number of disables and disables treated in each households, treatment.

*Seasonal Analysis*

— Identify the various health problems and remedies used.
— List the health problems and the months over the year it is faced. Record local remedies used.

*Example*:

| *Health Problems* | *Months* | *Remedies* |
|---|---|---|
| Diarrhoea | Chaita, Baishakh, Jeth (*March to June*) | Nun, Chini, Pani (*Salt, Sugar, Water*) |

*Agriculture Programme*

Explain the village map:

1. Indicate the households, using high yielding varieties.
2. Identify and list the varieties of major cereal crops used in the area. Identify the sources of seed. If the source is within village indicate the household and outside village record the source.
3. Record the proportion of the land of each household under high yielding varieties.
4. Indicate the households using chemical fertilizer and improved compost using separate symbols.
5. Identify the methods of pre—and post—harvest loss control. Record the proportion of households using this method, down according to villagers.
6. Record the proportion of households with improved breeds.
7. Identify the sources of improved breeds.
8. Record the proportion of households with fodder grass and trees planted.
9. Identify the sources of seeds/seedlings of fodder.
10. Record the proportion of farmers getting help from agriculture and livestock assistants.
11. Record the proportion of farmers getting help from AAN agriculture organizer.
12. Indicate the households having kitchen garden and fruit trees using separate symbols.
13. Indicate the forest users' groups (distinguish the registered and non-registered groups)
14. Record the total area of irrigated land from AAN irrigation scheme in local measuring units.
15. make note on increase in production and number of crops. Indicate the households benefitting from the irrigation scheme.
16. Record all irrigation canals existing in the village.

*Income Generation (IG) Programmes*

1. Explain the village map.
2. Indicate the following on the map:
   - — Household with person received IG training.
   - — Number of persons in each households using the skills and having production training.
   - — Household with production from other IG support except training.
   - — Households with their production selling.
     - * household selling their production individually.
     - * household selling their production through group.
     - * household selling their production to AAN.
   - — Make a circle on the map to identify households in each IG group.
   - — Households using loan; give separate symbols for different sources of loan

3. Record following on a separate sheet using HH number and heads name:
   - — Volume of production and annual income.
   - — Per unit price.
   - — Amount and purpose of loan.
4. Record the discussion on the market facilities and the price of their products; whether they are sold at reasonable price or not.

*Some Practical Tips for Survey*

1. Don't concentrate with one person in dialogue. Bring in all the participants.
2. Don't repeat the same question, rephrase it if not understood.
3. Don't rush. Let the villagers flow in their expression.
4. Don't limit yourself to the fact and figures, listen to their opinions.
5. Don't limit yourself in planned structure, discuss the things suited to situation.
6. Don't ask closed questions, Ask open—ended questions.
7. Listen. Don't lecture the villagers.

*Recording Information*

1. Don't secretly write in your note book.
2. Put your paper on place where everybody could see.
3. Write things only after confirming it with the villagers.
4. Start with question how to draw village map. Let the villagers draw it:
   - Give responsibility to villagers.
   - Set such a climate that a person drawing map listens to the comments made on map.
   - Let all people see the map drawing.
   - Use sticks to draw lines, better if it is on ground with sand.
   - Use easily available materials like stones, grains etc. as visuals to indicate things on map numbers".

## A-2

# Extracts from Haddad *et al.* (1993): 'Alternative Methods to Locate the Food and Nutrition Insecure', IFPRI-ICRISAT-APAU, February.

## "Village Mapping in Rounds 2 and 3 in Shirapur and Aurepalle

### Objectives

To identify households that the community perceives to be (i) 'very high risk' and (ii) at 'no risk' of food and nutrition insecurity. By 'high risk' we mean families which struggle to provide enough food for their families.

The criteria for selection into these two groups will be determined by the villagers in this exercise. *Do not lead the group by using your own criteria to define high and low risk families.* Instead, use the local terms written in the protocol below:

*1.1 Instructions for Completing the Village Map Identification with Male Subjects*

We will not be able to fit a whole village onto a single map. Therefore in Aurepalle and Shirapur it will be necessary to draw several 'sub-maps' of the villagers. The 'sub–maps' should be of neighbourhoods within the village which are small enough that villagers are familiar with all the households and all the facilities available in the area (e.g. water pumps, shops etc.). . . . Please follow these steps for each sub-map drawn:

(1) A few days before the map is to be drawn, randomly select 2 groups (10-20), one of men and one of women from the village (they do not have to be from survey households). Visit each member of the group and explain what you would like them to participate in. If they agree to help draw the map, arrange a time and place that is good for everyone in the group to meet in a few days to draw the

map. Make sure that the place you choose is cool and comfortable.

(2) On the first visit in round 2 try to keep the number of participants to a manageable number (but do not turn people away). Have the villagers draw a complete map of their neighborhood. Make sure that all survey households are covered in the sub-map. *It is important to include all structures (not just houses) that the villagers think are important to them.* It is not important to do a census of all the people in the village for this exercise, so do not go through the process of painstakingly identifying all individuals in each household.

(3) At the end of the exercise either you or one of the villagers should copy the map onto paper.

(4) When you get back to the office draw, make a copy of the map so that you have 2 paper copies.

(5) In the *next week, return to the village* with 1 map on paper for a larger group of *male* villagers to:

   (a) *check the accuracy of the map* (i.e. that no household has been left off) and

   (b) identify households which are "very high risk" and "no risk"

** ** **

(6) On the proforma, record which houses have been identified as 'high risk'. For each house, record as much information as possible as to why each of the households is considered at 'very high risk'. Write this in the comments section. In the box below this record general observations on why households are considered at 'no risk' by the villagers. *Pay attention to disagreements,* and why they arise. Also note if there is overwhelming consensus on the *emic reasons for classifying households into either of these categories.*

*1.2 Instructions for Completing the Village Map Identification with Female Subjects:*

(1) Repeat steps (1)-(6) for a group of female villagers. Do not show the female villagers the map from the male group until the women have finished identifying 'very at risk' and 'no risk' households. If the male versus female versions differ make sure you probe to determine the source of these differences.

While doing this please remember that this exercise is designed to find out about local perceptions about the village. Therefore, if you find discrepancies between the male and female maps, do not attempt to get the group to 'correct' them. Rather, probe gently and neutrally to find out why they have shown something the way that they have.

(2) In round 3, bring the maps from round 2 and update them by checking on the status of the households identified as at 'very high risk' and 'no risk' in round 2. Has their situation improved or deteriorated? Why? Note any new households that have moved into the village. Pay particular attention to any households that have gone from 'no-risk' in the round 2 to 'very high risk' in round 3, and *vice versa.*

## FORM

| Village Map Recording Form | Group:———— (1 = male, 2 = female) |
|---|---|

| Date: | Round: | Village Code: | |
|---|---|---|---|
| Time started the map activity: | | | |
| Activity Director: | | | |
| Data Recorder(s): | | | |
| Other project observer(s): | | | |
| Enumerator Code of Activity Director: | | | |
| Enumerator Code(s) of Data Recorder: | | | |
| Names of persons who drew the map: | | | |
| Time Ended the map activity: | | | |

| IDENTIFICATION OF 'VERY HIGH RISK AND LOW RISK HOUSEHOLDS' EXERCISE (Page 1): | | |
|---|---|---|
| Specific comments on why each household is identified as "very high risk" | | |
| Name of Household Head | Household ID number if in survey? | Comments on indicators of "very high risk" |
| | | |
| | | |
| | | |
| | | |
| | | |
| | | |
| | | |
| | | |
| | | |
| | | |
| | | |
| | | |
| | | |
| | | |
| | | |
| | | |

IDENTIFICATION OF 'VERY HIGH RISK AND LOW RISK HOUSEHOLDS' EXERCISE (Page 2):

Specific comments on why each household is identified as "very high risk"

| Name of Household Head | Household ID number if in survey? | Comments on indicators of "very high risk" |
|---|---|---|
| | | |
| | | |
| | | |
| | | |
| | | |
| | | |
| | | |
| | | |
| | | |
| | | |
| | | |
| | | |
| | | |
| | | |
| | | |
| | | |

| General comments on why households are identified as "no risk" of food insecurity: |
|---|
| |
| |
| |
| |
| |

| Time ended: |
|---|

| General comments on the Mapping Exercise: |
|---|
| |

# BIBLIOGRAPHY

ActionAid Nepal, (1992), Utilization Survey Report Part I, Rural Development Area, Sindhupal Chowk, Monitoring and Evaluation Unit, ActionAid Nepal, July.

Adams, Alayne, DasRoy, Rita, and Mahbub, Amina, (1993), "Participatory Methods to Assess Change in Health and Women's Lives: An Exploratory Study for the BRAC-ICDDR, September.

Bardhan, Pranab (ed.), (1989), *Conversations Between Economists and Anthropologists*, Oxford University Press, Oxford.

Beebe, J., (1985), Rapid Rural Appraisal; the critical first step in a farming systems approach to research, Farming Systems Support Project, Networking Paper No.5, 36 pages.

Breman, Jan, (1985), *Of Peasant, Migrants and Paupers: Rural Labour Circulation and Capitalist Production in West India*, Oxford University Press, Delhi.

Buchanan-Smith Margaret, Abdelkader Khadidja, Abdelmajid M. Saleh, Allemane Amos, Banguita Idriss, Behom, Djel Soudho, Idrissa Brahim, Kleih Ulrich, Mbailenang Boykas, Riviere Francois, Sainibi Alladoum, Tambayo Djeder, and Vandou Bagda, (1992), 'Finding Out How People Prioritise Their Food Security Problems In Chad: The Challenges Of RRA At National Level', Paper presented at the Institute of Development Studies, 30th January.

Bulmer, M and Warwick, D.P. (ed.) (1983), *Social Research in Developing Countries. Surveys and Censuses in the Third World*, John Wiley and Sons.

Casley, Denis and Kumar, Krishna, (1988), *The Collection, Analysis and Use of Monitoring and Evaluation Data*, Published for the World Bank by John Hopkins University Press, Baltimore.

Chambers, Robert, (1983), *Rural Development: Putting the Last First*, London, Longman.

Chambers, Robert, (1986), 'Poverty in India: Concepts, Research and Reality -an exploration', typescript, Institute of Development Studies, University of Sussex, Brighton, 22nd July.

Chambers, Robert, (1991), "Shortcut and Participatory Methods for gaining Social Information for Projects" in Cernea Michael M. (ed.) *Putting People First, Sociological Variables in Rural Development,* Oxford University Press.

Chambers, Robert, (1993), 'Participatory Rural Appraisal (PRA): Challenges, Potential And Paradigm', Institute of Development Studies, Sussex, July.

Chambers, Robert (1994), Participatory Rural Appraisal (PRA): Analysis of Experience, *World Development*, Vol. 22, No.9, pp.1253-1268.

Colfer, Carol J. Pierce, Agus, Fahmuddin, Gill, Dan, Sudjadi, M., Uehara, Goro & Wade, M.K., (1987), 'Farmer Involvement in the Tropsoils Project: Two Complementary Approaches' for the IDS Workshop on 'Farmers and Agricultural Research: Complementary Methods' at the Institute of Development Studies at the University of Sussex, 26-31 July.

Conlin, S., (1979), 'Baseline surveys: an escape from thinking about research problems and, even more, a refuge from actually doing anything', Rapid Rural Appraisal Conference, Institute of Development Studies, 4-7 December.

Connell, John and Lipton, Michael, (1973), Assessing Village Labour Situations in Developing Countries, Comparative Study of Aims, Concepts and Methods in Village Surveys bearing on Labour Utilisation, *IDS Discussion paper* no. 35, University of Sussex, U.K.

Farming Systems Research Unit, (1991) 'Structural Adjustment and Communal Area Agriculture, Case Studies from Mangwende and Chivi Communal Areas', Department of Research and Specialist Services, Ministry of Lands, Agriculture and Rural Resettlement, Harare, Zimbabwe, November.

Fowler, Floyd J. Jr. and Mangione, Thomas W., (1990) *Standardized Survey Interviewing, Minimizing Interviewer-Related Error* (Applied Social Research Methods Series, Volume 18) Beverly Hills, CA, Sage.

Franzel, Steven and Crawford, Eric W., (1987), 'Comparing Formal and Informal Survey Techniques for Farming Systems Research: A Case Study from Kenya', *Agricultural Administration and Extension,* Elsevier Applied Science Publishers Ltd., England.

Fry, P.H. and McCabe, J.T., (1986), 'A Comparison of Two Survey Methods on Pastoral Turkana Migration Patterns and the Implications for Development Planning', Pastoral Development Network, paper 22b, September, Agricultural Administration Unit, Overseas Development Network, Regent's College, London.

Gill, Gerard J., (1992), 'But How Does it compare with the Real Data', *RRA Notes*, Number 14, IIED, London.

Gill, Gerard J., (1992), *Policy Analysis for Agricultural Resource Management in Nepal: A Comparison of Conventional and Participatory Approaches*, Research Support Series, Number 9, HMG Ministry of Agriculture/Winrock International, Policy Analysis in Agriculture and Related Resource Management, July.

Gill, Gerry, (1993), O.K., The Data's Lousy, But Its All We've Got (Being a Critique of Conventional Methods), *Gatekeeper Series* No.38, Sustainable Agriculture Programme, International Institute of Environment and Development.

Guba, Egon G. (ed.), (1990), *The Paradigm Dialog*, Sage, California.

Gubrium, Jaber F. & Silverman, David, (ed.), (1989), *The Politics of Field Research-Sociology Beyond Enlightenment*, Sage, London.

Haddad, Lawrence, Chung, Kimberly and Devi, Yasoda P., (1993), "Alternative Methods to Locate the Food and Nutrition Insecure", Work in Progress in South India IFPRI-ICRISAT-APAU, February.

Hammersley, Martyn, (1992), *What's Wrong With Ethnography ?*, Routeledge, London.

Hoeper, Bernhard (compiled), (1991), *Qualitative Versus Quantitative Approaches in Applied Empirical Research in Rural Development* (A Documentation of the Workshop at Sokoine University of Agriculture, Morogoro/Tanzania, 21-26 May, 1990), Zed Books, Bonn.

Hubert, Jean-Pierre, (1991), "Comparing two methods for implementing Farming Systems Surveys in the Imbo Region of Burundi", 11th FSR/E Symposium, October 91, Michigan State University.

Hunt, Jennifer C., (1989), *Psychoanalytic Aspects of Fieldwork* (Sage University paper Series on Qualitative Research Methods, Volume 18), Beverly Hills, CA, Sage.

Hyman, Herbert, (1960), *Survey Design and Analysis: Principles, Cases and Procedures*, The Free Press Publishers, Glencoe, Illinois.

Inglis, Andy, (1991), Comparing RRA and Conventional Surveys in Local Forestry Knowledge of Sierra Leone, Edinburgh Centre for Tropical Forests.

Inglis, Andy, (1991), Harvesting Local Forestry Knowledge: A Comparison of RRA and Conventional Surveys, *RRA Notes*, IIED, London, Number 12, July.

Inglis, Andy, (1992), 'A Tale of Two Approaches: Conventional

Questionnaire Surveys Vs. PRA', Rural Development Forestry Network, Winter.

Johansson, Lars and Hoben, Allan, 'RRA's for land policy formulation in Tanzania', *Forests, Trees and People Newsletter No. 15/16.*

Katzer, Jeffrey, Cook, Kenneth H. and Crouch, Wayne W., (1982), *Evaluating Information, A Guide for Users of Social Science Research*, Addison Wesley Publishing Company, Philippines.

Khon Khan University, (1987), *Proceedings of 1985 International Conference on Rapid Rural Appraisal*, Rural Systems Research and Farming Systems Research Projects, Khon Kaen University, Khon Kaen, Thailand.

Lanjouw, Peter and Stern, Nicholas, (1991), 'Poverty in Palanpur', *The World Bank Economic Review*, Vol. 5, No.1: 23-55, The World Bank.

Lin, Nan, (1976), *Foundations of Social Research*, McGraw-Hill, New York.

Longhurst, Richard, (1993), 'Integrating Formal Sample Surveys and Rapid Rural Appraisal Techniques', Centre for International Child Health, Institute of Child Health, University of London, June.

Luning, H.A., (1986), 'Survey Integration Comes of Age', Inaugural Address delivered at the International Institute for Aerospace Survey and Earth Sciences (ITC), Enschede, on Thursday, 9th January.

Malik, Humeira and Richard, Edwards, (1993/94) (Notes and pers. comm.), Large Scale Wealth Ranking in West Pakistan: An Application by ActionAid, Pakistan.

McCracken, Grant, (1988), *The Long Interview* (Sage University paper Series on Qualitative Research Methods, Volume 13), Beverly Hills, CA, Sage.

Morgan, David, (1988), *Focus Groups as Qualitative Research* (Sage University Paper Series on qualitative Research Methods, Vol.16), Beverly Hills, CA, Sage.

Moris, Jon R., (1970), 'Multi-Subject Farm Surveys Reconsidered: Some Methodological Lessons', East African Agricultural Economics Society Conference, Dar es Salem, 31st March 1970 to 4th April.

Mukherjee, Neela, (1993), *Participatory Rural Appraisal: Methodology and Applications,* Concept Publishing Company, Delhi.

National Council of Applied Economic Research, (1992), *Evaluating the Impact of Commercialisation of Rural Dairy Sector: An Application of RRA Technique*, New Delhi.

National Council of Applied Economic Research, (1993), *Comparative Study of Sample Survey and Participatory Rural Appraisal Methodologies with special reference to evaluation of national programme on improved chullah*, November, Delhi.

Nichols, Paul, (1991), *Social Survey Methods, A Fieldguide for Development Workers*, Oxfam, Oxford.

Pretty, N. Jules, (1993), "Alternative Systems of Inquiry for a Sustainable Agriculture", Sustainable Agriculture Programme, International Institute for Environment and Development, London, 10th December, 1993.

Pottier Johan, (1991), 'Representation and Accountability : Understanding Social Change Through Rapid Appraisal with reference to Northern Zambia', Department of Social Anthropology, S.O.A.S., University of London.

Rajaratnam, Jolly, Ganeshan, C., Thasian, Helen, Babu, Navamoni, Abel, Rajaratnam, (1992), *Validating Wealth Ranking of PRA and Formal Survey in Identifying the Rural Poor*, RUHSA Department, Christian Medical College and Hospital, RUHSA Campus, 632209, North Arcot Ambedkar District, Tamil Nadu, South India, April.

Scherr, Sara, Vosti, Steve and Haddad, Lawrence, (1992), 'Theoretical and Conceptual Issues of Data Needs: Towards Criteria for Choice of Approaches', Paper presented to International Workshop on 'Data Needs for Food Policy in Developing Countries: Directions for Household Survey', International Food Policy Research Institute, Washington, D.C., September 1-2.

Schwandt, Thomas R., (1990), "Paths to Inquiry in the Social Disciplines-Scientific, Constructivist and Critical Theory Methodologies", in Guba Egon G. (ed.) *The Paradigm Dialog*, Sage, California.

Shah, Parmesh, (1993), 'Questionnaires: Participatory, Reliable and Interesting ?' A note prepared for IIED/IDS workshop on 'Alternatives to Questionnaire surveys' on 26th October.

Stegeman, G.T., (1991), 'Community Participatory Forestry For Fuelwood Production In The Western Area, Sierra Leone, Socio-Economic Baseline Survey for 10 Villages, Ministry of Agriculture, Natural Resources and Forestry FAO, Freetown, February.

Streiffeler, Friedhelm, (1990), 'Qualitative Versus Quantitative Methods in Social Sciences Research', in Hoeper Bernhard (compiled) *Qualitative Versus Quantitative Approaches in Applied Empirical Research in Rural Development*, Zed, Bonn.

UNICEF Video: "The Pressure of Fact: Community Based Sentinel Surveys", VHS, UNICEF.

Vaidyanathan, A., (1989), 'Macro and Micro Approaches to Studying Rural Economic Change: Some Pointers from Indian Experience' in Bardhan, Pranab (ed.), *Conversations Between Economists and Anthropologists,* Oxford University Press, Oxford.

Warren, Michael D. and Cashman Kristin, (1989), Indigenous Knowledge for Sustainable Agriculture and Rural Development, Gatekeeper Series No. SA 10, Sustainable Agriculture Programme, IIED, London.

World, Fertility Survey, (1975 and 1977), Core Questionnaire and Modifications, basic documentation Nos. 1 and 10, London.

Zafar, Rosanah, (1993), 'Water, Sanitation, Environment and Development, Evolution of a Participatory Research Methodology', 19th WEDC Conference, Accra, Ghana.

Ziche, Joachim (1990), 'Some Critical Aspects in Gathering Socio-economic Data in Rural Areas of Non-Western Societies' in Hoeper, Bernhard (compiled) (1990) *Qualitative Versus Quantitative Approaches in Applied Empirical Research in Rural Development*, Zed Publishers, Bonn.

# INDEX